The Ex-Boyfriend Cookbook

THE EX-BOYFRIEND COOKBOOK

They Came, They Cooked, They Left
(But We Ended Up with Some Great Recipes)

ERIN ERGENBRIGHT AND THISBE NISSEN

HarperResource
An Imprint of HarperCollinsPublishers

HarperCollins books may be purchased for educational, business, or sales promotional use. For information, please write to: Special Markets Department, HarperCollins Publishers Inc., 10 East 53rd Street, New York, New York 10022.

FIRST EDITION

DESIGN BY RENATO STANISIC

Library of Congress Cataloging-in-Publication Data

Ergenbright, Erin.
    The ex-boyfriend cookbook: they came, they cooked, they left (but we ended up with some great recipes) / Erin Ergenbright and Thisbe Nissen.— 1st ed.
        p. cm.
ISBN 0-06-018520-1
    I. Nissen, Thisbe, 1972-II. Title.

TX652 .E595 2002
641.5—dc21   2001024496

02 03 04 05 06 IM 10 0 9 7 6 5 4 3 2 1

Printed in Singapore

To all the men we've loved before . . .

ACKNOWLEDGMENTS

Erin and Thisbe want to send thanks to the many friends who have lent their images, stories and recipes to this project: to Eric Simonoff (without whose support and dedication this book would not have happened), Ayesha Pande, Nick Darrell, Harriet Bell, Megan Newman, Leah Carlson-Stanisic, Karen Lumley, Diane Aronson, and Matthew Benjamin at HarperCollins, and Martin at Copyman, who saw this project through its beginning and many incarnations. Grateful thanks to Ric, Jill, Dana and Megan Ergenbright; Myra and Tony Nissen; Evan Shopper and Debbie Zeidenberg; Katie Hubert and Kimberly Langford; Christin Quissell; Bruce Skinner; Colleen Veltz; Jeff Hansen; Vito Dilullo; Dave Holstrom for his fabulous quiche; Auntie Jan for her oatmeal raisin cookie recipe.

Also thanks to: David Wells and the fantastic mushroom story, which we promptly distorted; Tami Mansfield; Mitchell Harris; Scott Rasmussen; Stiv Wilson; Vicki Tolar Burton; Kevin Larimer; Colin Meloy and the boys who posed for pictures on the warehouse roof; Brandon Brown; Cindy Jo Wavra; Phil Landis; Sebastian Lapostol; Steven Burnett; Zephyr Copies in Iowa City; Krista Bartz; Jacques Massey; Laurel Snyder; Allison Amend; Matt Miller; the Workshop softball players; Robin Beck's mom for her cream cheese brownies; Cara Wall; Justin Tussing and his smoked turkey; Patricia Lawrence for her quesadilla thingies; Will Halby for his subtitles; everyone in Ms. Mayberry's nursery class; folks from Hunter High School; the folks at Evan and Deb's wedding; the girls of Banana House; Sarah Townsend and the Iowa Contingent; Seth Harwood; Josh Emmons; Chris Dimond; Sandy Dyas for Tasha and for continuing inspiration; the cats: Fernanda, Maisie, Sinclair and Lucy; Grandpa Nissen and his horse, Maude; and Nana Belle for her soup and Passover cake. Special thanks to Heather Krebsbach and Erin Graham for enduring Erin's bad housekeeping during the last weeks of this project; Erin's co-workers at Southpark who covered her shifts when she needed to write; and, of course, the boys whose memories and quirks made this book possible.

Contents

INTRODUCTION

It's amazing the reactions you get when you tell people you're writing an ex-boyfriend cookbook.

"What?" asked our friend Lisa, skeptically. "Like how to fricassee the ones who really pissed you off?"

"Not a how-to-cook-your-ex-boyfriend cookbook," we told her. "A book of recipes we've gotten from ex-boyfriends over the years."

"You've dated men who could cook?" Allison asked, incredulous.

"Great," Jane cried, "a cookbook with nothing but recipes for toast and ice cubes!"

"If you were lucky," Jen muttered under her breath.

So, maybe we are a little jaded, but we've honestly been served some damn fine meals. And we've dated some pretty amazing cooks. Chefs in New York restaurants, short-order fry cooks, campfire cooks, that guy who worked the waffle line at Campus Dining Service. One ex-boyfriend baked bread whenever he got depressed. Another worked in an upscale gourmet food store where the owners paid him minimum wage and he felt compelled (and thoroughly justified) to steal copious amounts of absurdly expensive produce, spices and condiments with which he'd concoct heavenly dinners in the kitchen of the run-down boardinghouse where he lived with eleven impoverished housemates, six flea-riddled cats and a parrot named Igor.

It's likely that everyone could make a list of things gained and lost in relationships—material, spiritual, physical, intellectual. We take away from relationships all sorts of things: perfectly worn-in Levi's, those mixes with lots of REM and Peter Gabriel that they make for us during the gushy phases, espresso makers we've bought together, personal insights, new pet peeves, a list of character flaws to watch out for in men we might date sometime in the future. We gain weight, gain religion, gain great and profound understandings of human interaction in the world. We lose things to relationships as well: virginity, innocence, pride, CDs, hardcover autographed first editions of out-of-print books by our favorite authors, thousands of dollars in long-distance phone bills, years of our lives, years *off* our lives. Coming out of failed relationships makes us lose weight, lose self-respect, lose countless hours to therapy.

People have written all sorts of books about the things lost and gained in relationships. There have certainly been plenty of books on women who give too much, on men who give too little, on people who give the exact right amount of all the wrong things. But in our experience we've never come across a book of what we find to be one of the most valuable things one takes away from relationships: recipes.

We aren't scoffing at love—not at all! We're actually about the biggest romantic cheesebags (no, that's not the name of a dish, it's an expression) we've ever known. This is not a renunciation of love, but a celebration of the search for it and the things we share with another person during that search. Specifically, food.

These are *our* ex-boyfriend recipe stories. If you're anything like our friends, we're sure you all have plenty of your own. Once you tell people you're writing an ex-boyfriend cookbook, suddenly everyone's got a story to tell you. So we've left you a few pages in the back on which you can add some of your own ex-boyfriend recipes—and recipes of ex-boyfriends yet to come. We're not, nor have we ever been, married ourselves, thus there are no ex-husband recipes, but if you've got one, please feel free to include it, along with any ex-girlfriend, ex-fiancé or ex-anything recipes.

All names have been changed to protect the guilty, the innocent, the ones we're not yet over, the ones who haven't gotten over us and the ones who don't yet know they're exes. We run great risk in putting these recipes out into the world, namely, that no one will ever want to date us again for fear of winding up as an index listing for potato kugel. Or worse: that the men we date will refuse to cook for us, or that we'll have to sign predining agreements swearing never to release the ingredients of the food we are about to consume.

Nonetheless, here they are. And like the men who made them, these recipes are varied and run the gamut of our romantic histories, from pathological liars to Ph.D. candidates in Ancient Greek civilization to the sweet little boy next door. We hope you enjoy them as much as we have.

Rob Becker's Mom's Cream Cheese Brownies

Brandon Fishbine's Grandmother's Oatmeal Cookies

Liam's Refrigerator Cookies

Theo the Thespian's Mother's Lace Cookies

Clarence's Far-out Frozen Peanut Butter Pie

The Orchard Boy's Berry Cobbler

Sweet Things

Arthur's Easy Apple Dessert

Edward's English Toffee

Fickle Vance's Brownies

Sam's Apple Crisp

David Goldberg's Flourless Chocolate Torte

Murphy the Folksinger's Apple Pie

Derrick Vandernagle's Mother's
Chocolate Chip Cookies

ROB BECKER'S MOM'S CREAM CHEESE BROWNIES

To our senior prom Rob wore a silver cummerbund to match my dress: silver stretch sequins. I ruined the dress later in the evening rolling around at Jones Beach with one of the waiters. Rob told people we broke up because we were going to different colleges, and who could handle the long-distance thing really, and besides he knew I needed to play the field a little before I'd be ready to settle down with anyone. He was considerate like that, always looking out for my best interests. Rob's a market analyst now: married, three kids, drives a sport-utility vehicle through Manhattan rush hour traffic—but it's Rob's mom who never really got over our breakup. All through college she carried a torch for me, and twice a year, at exam time, sent me a care package of these brownies. I am one of the only people to whom she's released this recipe—so that I could bake them for Rob when we got married.

> 6 ounces cream cheese, softened (don't even think of using fat-free or lite—the results are nasty)
> 5 tablespoons butter, softened (BUTTER. Period. Not margarine, not oil, not Crisco, not "spread," not "I can't believe this isn't what it's supposed to be . . .")
> 1/3 cup granulated sugar
> 2 eggs (the kind that only chickens lay, please)
> 2 tablespoons flour
> 3/4 teaspoon vanilla extract
> 1 package family-size fudge brownie mix

Preheat the oven to 350°F.
Cream cheese mixture: beat together the cream cheese and

butter. Add the sugar, eggs, flour and vanilla. Beat until smooth. Set aside.

Prepare the brownies according to the instructions on the box for "cakelike" brownies.

Spread half the batter into the bottom of a greased 9 × 13-inch pan. Pour the entire cream cheese mixture over it. Spoon the rest of the brownie mixture in dollops over the cream cheese (i.e., don't cover it completely with brownie batter). Swirl the layers together by drawing squiggles through with the tip of a knife or spatula.

Bake for 36 to 39 minutes.

Brandon Fishbine's Grandmother's Oatmeal Cookies

Brandon was my tenth-grade boyfriend, and I was drawn to him mainly because he dyed his hair a new color every week and often wore mismatched shoes. He was the kind of guy who could pull off nearly anything and make it look easy.

Unfortunately, he died.

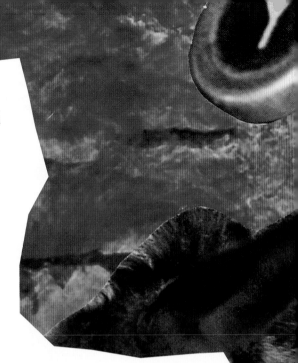

1 cup sifted flour
$^1/_2$ teaspoon baking soda
$^1/_2$ teaspoon salt
1 teaspoon cinnamon
$^1/_4$ teaspoon nutmeg
$^1/_2$ cup butter, softened
$^1/_2$ cup brown sugar
$^1/_2$ cup granulated sugar
1 egg
2 tablespoons milk
$^1/_2$ cup raisins
2 cups uncooked oats
1 cup chopped nuts

Preheat the oven to 375°F. Sift the dry ingredients. Add a mixture of softened butter and sugars, egg and milk. Beat until smooth—about 2 minutes. Fold in the raisins, oats and nuts.

Drop from a teaspoon onto a greased cookie sheet (old ones work best) and bake for 10 minutes.

LIAM'S REFRIGERATOR COOKIES

Liam had the most frightening refrigerator I've ever beheld. Not only were there many containers of unrecognizable substances and a carton of eggs he claimed had been there since he moved in, but also the carcasses of several small animals that he wanted to dissect.

After a few months of dating I decided to clean out Liam's refrigerator. No amount of whining or badgering could make *him* clean it, so I borrowed a gas mask from my vet neighbor, bought two bottles of 409 and rubber gloves, and went to work. It took two hours and three sponges to turn the refrigerator back into an acceptable repository for food, but I actually enjoyed myself, likening the process to growing up, throwing things away that were rotten or no longer needed. It was exhilarating to enact such change. The only thing I didn't throw away was a roll of frozen cookie dough that had been wrapped in foil and placed inside two Ziploc bags. I unwrapped the roll, let it thaw a bit, sliced it and baked some cookies.

When Liam came home that day and smelled the combination of cookies and 409, he freaked out. "I'm an adult! I don't need anyone to take care of me!" he bellowed. He said some other mean things about my cats and my haircut, and that was that. It was over.

I never beg in relationships (okay, maybe once), but I begged with all my might for the cookie recipe. By some miracle (actually, it was the agreement that I would give him my electric pencil sharpener, which he'd always loved) he acquiesced and now this recipe is my very own. I'm sharing it, and you can even keep your electric pencil sharpener. Those things never really work anyway.

1 cup brown sugar
1 cup granulated sugar
1 cup melted shortening
4 cups flour
1 cup chopped walnuts
2 teaspoons baking powder
4 eggs, well beaten
2 teaspoons cinnamon
1 teaspoon vanilla extract

Preheat the oven to 350°F. Mix the ingredients and form dough into two rolls. Wrap in plastic wrap and put in the freezer overnight (or as long as you want). Unwrap, slice thinly and bake for 10 minutes. Yummy!

THEO THE THESPIAN'S MOTHER'S LACE COOKIES

I did a lot of theater in high school, spent most weekends and Christmas vacations holed up in the auditorium rehearsing some corny musical, complaining gleefully and more or less constantly about having to be there in the first place, and savoring every campy, choreographed minute. Rehearsals were especially glorious when I happened to be in love with one fellow cast member or another, such as the season I spent mooning over the incomparable Theo as we prepared our production of *Bye Bye Birdie*. He, of course, was in love with the nymphet playing Kim, and I was thus able to indulge in the mortal anguish of my unrequited love. Which is to say: this is his mother's recipe for lace cookies that he baked once and brought to rehearsal. My unrelenting pursuit of this recipe did nothing by way of getting Theo to fall in love with me, but the cookies are really good, and it did give me something to focus on for a while aside from just being a teenager and loathing myself. And I guess we do have to be thankful for small favors.

Beat together

1/2 cup granulated sugar

1/2 cup brown sugar

1 cup quick-cooking oats

1/2 teaspoon salt

1 tablespoon flour

1 egg, well beaten

1/2 teaspoon vanilla extract

Preheat oven to 325° or 350°F.

Cover a cookie sheet with aluminum foil and drop the batter on in teaspoonfuls. Flatten them a little.

Bake until golden brown. Cool, and peel from the foil.

CLARENCE'S FAR-OUT FROZEN PEANUT BUTTER PIE

Dating an astrologer who has studied your chart is a little strange because he will understand, or be able to explain, anything you do as being preordained, or destined in the stars. It's a little like buying one of those stupid daily astrology calendars that tell you that on

February 2nd you'll get in a fight with your roommate and then spending that entire day determined not to fight. There are some things you shouldn't know, really, until they happen. One can affect history (positively or negatively) with too much knowledge, and though it works in the movies, in real life it can be bad, bad, bad.

Clarence was eventually a little too intuitive for his own good, though his gift meant that the meals he prepared were the exact things I craved on a particular day, and the things he said desperately needed to be said, and at that specific moment. And soon, as psychology might suggest, I started lying to him, determined not to feel the way he thought I should feel, or to want the things he knew I wanted. But I will never be able to deny loving this frozen peanut butter pie. It *will* cure what ails you. Momentarily, anyway.

    4 ounces cream cheese
    1 cup powdered sugar
    1/3 cup peanut butter
    1/2 cup milk
    4 Reese's peanut butter cups, crushed
    1 cup heavy cream, whipped
    One 9-inch baked graham cracker crust

Beat the cheese until soft and fluffy. Beat in the sugar and peanut butter. Add the milk, blending thoroughly. Fold in the crushed peanut butter cups and whipped cream. Pour into the crust, and freeze until firm.

THE ORCHARD BOY'S BERRY COBBLER

During berry season, the second summer I worked at the farm in Virginia (See Lucas Amarati's Gazpacho and the Legend of Beet Man in Savory Things), I was selling our daily pickings of blueberries and strawberries at a farmers' market in Tacoma Park, Maryland, when the guy working the stand next to ours asked me if I wanted to do a swap. He was from an orchard further south, and he had some of the loveliest peaches I'd seen. He knew a fabulous recipe for berry cobbler, and proceeded to write it down for me during a particularly slow stretch in the selling day. We traded blueberries for peaches, and packed up our trucks and drove back to our respective farms. I never saw him again, but he is forever immortalized by this cobbler.

Mix together

8 cups blueberries, raspberries, strawberries or peaches

1 1/2 cups sugar

1/4 cup flour

2 tablespoons grated lemon zest

Spoon the mixture into a buttered baking dish.

To make the topping, mix
$1/2$ cup sugar
1 $3/4$ cups flour
2 teaspoons baking soda
$1/2$ teaspoon salt
1 stick (4 ounces) butter, cut
    into eighths

Preheat the oven to 375°F.
  Mush together until coarsely blended, then add one beaten egg and sprinkle mixture on top of berry mixture. Bake for 45 minutes to an hour. Serve with ice cream.

ARTHUR'S EASY APPLE DESSERT

When Arthur decided to drop out of college and travel to New Zealand to work in an organic apple orchard, I was sad but not hurt. There were things he needed to do, and his needs were different from mine, his wanderlust more far-reaching. I would never have wanted him to stay and put his dreams on hold for me, and I wouldn't have wanted to be with someone who'd put me above himself that way. It still seems tragic though, because I think maybe we could have loved each other. We have lost touch, as I suppose is inevitable, but sometimes I imagine that our paths might cross again. Maybe it's only because I knew him for such a short time that I can deposit him so effortlessly into my future. Almost an unknown, he is the perfect empty vessel, and I have been able, over the years, to create him again and again as the man who might finally be right in every way that the others have always been wrong.

3 Granny Smith apples
Juice of 1/2 lemon
1/4 cup cognac or bourbon
1/4 pound unsalted butter
3/4 cup brown sugar
1/4 cup granulated sugar
3/4 cup flour

Preheat the oven to 350°F.

Peel and core the apples. Cut into thin slices. Arrange in a buttered, ovenproof baking dish. Sprinkle lemon juice over the apples. Pour the alcohol over the apples. With fingers, cream together the remaining ingredients and spread over the apples. Bake for 1 hour.

PAR
AVION

New Zealand
Hukereteke Falls

La Polynésie française

POSTE
BORA-BORA

PLEASE FORWARD?

TIBBE NISSEN

SOUTH ST.

POSTA

SORRY ALL YOUR PICTURES
DID NOT COME OUT
HAPPY YOU DON'T HAVE TO
PAY FOR THE BAD ONES.
USE THIS CREDIT CARD FOR **2** PRINTS
PLEASE SEND 15c FOR HANDLING

72643

72643

GLOBE TICKET CO.   (5) 260

the clouds
far away between the

NEED I SAY MORE?

SOUTHERN EDGE
CARDS
PHY and
RESH

Barrington
e spa

New Zealand KIWIFRUIT
The world's finest

TOOK FERRY ACROSS
MUCH

DROVE
THE ROADS
NEW ZEALAND

and all. Now

fiji

fiji

6c

50c

Sonia Island Village

NELSON FAST POST
5 PM
5 APR
1993
NZ

19 NEW ZEALAND 30s

$1.50

FIJI

NISSEN

LLE NISSEN
2844

15

EDWARD'S ENGLISH TOFFEE

When I moved from my studio apartment into a one-bedroom three floors up, I quickly realized that my new neighbor was my ex-boyfriend Edward's new girlfriend. Actually they weren't that new, just new to me.

I rarely *saw* Edward, although every Monday and Wednesday afternoon (my days off) I heard him with Annabelle through the thin walls. No matter how badly things have gone, how clear it is that you need never speak to someone again, to *hear* him with someone else is difficult. Take a moment to imagine it; not fun.

I had mostly forgotten this boy—a sweet, misguided painter—but faced with these intimate sounds, I felt oddly jealous and irritated. I wrote a few melancholy poems on Mondays and Wednesdays, drank a lot of cheap wine and reflected on the few really cool things Edward and I had done together.

Once we'd hiked to Carson Hot Springs after dark with two bottles of good wine and stayed the night, drinking and talking and risking the $500 fine for crossing the government-owned suspension bridge across the Wind River. Another time we rode our mountain bikes to the top of Dimple Hill in early summer. Ants, itchy weeds, our attempts at improvisational poetry and Edward's sweet mouth make up the montage of that excursion. It's impossible to sum up any relationship without slighting either party, so I won't even attempt it. The tangible thing that remains is, once again, a recipe, and this toffee will truly make you the darling of any potluck or office party.

1 cup pecans
1 pound butter
2 cups sugar
3 plain Hershey's chocolate bars

Grease a large, flat pan and sprinkle the pecans over the entire surface. Melt the butter in a heavy skillet; add the sugar gradually, stirring constantly with a wooden spoon. At first, the butter will be on top and the sugar on the bottom, then it will mix and look like thick gravy, then separate again and turn a light brown. When it comes together again, it's done. Pour immediately over the pecans. Melt the chocolate over hot water and spread on top of the candy. Let cool, and then break the candy into pieces with a small mallet (fun!).

FICKLE VANCE'S BROWNIES

I've been accused of being fickle (okay, I've *been* fickle) since I was fifteen, but I never truly understood the damage done by easily shifted attentions until I met another fickle person, with whom I fell into a sort of love thing. Though I could have sought comfort in the fact that it didn't really have anything to do with me (a fickle person has emotions that run like a faulty faucet—who knows what causes that unexpected shift from hot to cold?), I couldn't suppress wondering *what if I had done things differently*? Part of the attraction felt toward fickleness is what people playing the lottery feel: hope, expectation and the knowledge that the odds are against you. If you lose, no big deal. You knew, underneath the imagined prize, that it was never yours. A not-fickle person courting a fickle person feels they are performing a public service—they are trying to change a dangerous pattern, to reform someone to the accepted modes of relating. And it's funny that they are the very person a fickle person hopes for and dreams of: they are possibly *the one* who will rescue them from a ridiculous life of disappointing love affairs.

Then again, the stable and actualized nature of those people does not jibe with the nature of a fickle person. It's an endless and ultimately unsatisfying dance, and in dance, unless you're watching reruns of *Solid Gold* or *Dance Fever*, there is no winner. But . . . enough psychobabble. By now you know that obtaining an amazing brownie recipe is not truly enough to assuage a broken heart, but it's *something*.

$3^1/_2$ squares semisweet chocolate, melted
2 cups sugar
$^2/_3$ cup oil
4 eggs
$1^1/_2$ cups flour
1 teaspoon baking powder
1 tablespoon corn syrup
1 teaspoon vanilla extract

Mix the ingredients and bake in a 9×9-inch pan at 325°F for 25 minutes. Turn off the oven. Cover the brownies with 1 package miniature marshmallows, then melt together $1^1/_2$ squares semisweet chocolate, 1 stick butter and 1 box powdered sugar. Add enough evaporated milk to make spreading easy, and spread over the marshmallow layer. These brownies will satisfy the grumpiest, most premenstrual woman in the world.

2 cups milk
2 slightly beaten
Cook until this be

Into this hot mix

med sized jar M.cherries(cut u
1 cup walnuts meats(cut up)

old into c led custard
re k up ½   angel fo
pa pan (ake the

Since I
rs. Botti
as to hav
box for he
I am ass
for the ot
please des

Ber

Sam's Apple Crisp

Sam dug ditches, drank copious amounts of Budweiser and played a mean game of pool. He also told wonderful stories about castles and vampires, memorized Keats's poems and loved Tori Amos. He had a beauty mark on his cheek like a painted Parisian can-can girl's, smooth, pale skin and a rather reckless love for things illegal.

Before he went to prison, Sam was a regular at a small Iowa bar in a small Iowa town where I worked and which occupies much of my memory. Sam had such imagination, such passion and sadness, such hopelessness and hope it made me dizzy. We kissed, once, outside the Spotted Cow, our shoes sticking in the mud, our hair full of smoke. In rural Iowa the world moves slowly, but it stopped that night; the whirring generators and pulsing grain elevators were silenced, the heat lightning reduced to a flicker of white.

Sam didn't eat, really, but he once made me this amazing apple crisp and watched me eat it. At the time of this writing he didn't have access to this recipe, but I called his mother and she was able to find it for me.

$1^1/2$ pounds tart cooking apples
1 stick (4 ounces) butter or margarine
$3/4$ cup packed brown sugar
$3/4$ cup quick-cooking oatmeal
$1/2$ cup flour
1 teaspoon cinnamon

Preheat the oven to 350°F. Pare the apples; quarter, core and slice thinly. Arrange the slices in a buttered, shallow 6-cup baking dish. Melt the butter in a medium saucepan. Stir in the brown sugar, oatmeal, flour and cinnamon until the mixture is crumbly; sprinkle over the apples.

Bake for 35 minutes, or until the apples are soft. Serve warm with vanilla ice cream.

DAVID GOLDBERG'S FLOURLESS CHOCOLATE TORTE

David was like Whitman, a man of contradictions: he was complex; he contained multitudes. An Earth First!-er who smoked Salem Menthols, he read poetry and wanted to join the navy, thought "footsie" was distasteful but liked to have sex in McDonald's rest rooms, and hated cats but once owned a ferret. Perhaps it's needless to say that our relationship, such as it was, didn't last particularly long. Just long enough to get this recipe for Passover cake out of him.

  6 eggs, separated
  3/4 cup brown sugar
  1 cup chopped nuts
  4 ounces grated chocolate, semisweet (you can use chocolate
      chips and grate them in the food processor if that's easier)
  2 Delicious apples, grated
  1/2 cup matzoh meal
  3/4 teaspoon almond extract

Pre-heat the oven to 350°F.

Beat the egg yolks with the sugar until thick.

Stir in the nuts, chocolate, apples, matzoh meal and almond extract.

Beat the egg whites until stiff, but not dry. Using a rubber spatula, fold gently, but thoroughly, into the egg yolk mixture.

Turn the mixture into a 9-inch springform pan and bake for 45 minutes to an hour.

$$\frac{B\omega \cdot (B\omega)_c}{\omega^2 - \omega_c^2} d\omega$$

23

MURPHY THE FOLKSINGER'S APPLE PIE

Murphy came through town to play a gig at the local coffeehouse, and when he walked onto the stage, my entire body went pins-and-needles numb. I was mesmerized. He was the most beautiful, most talented, most astounding human being I had ever encountered. I couldn't feel my fingers. My leg started twitching. At the set break, unable to stop myself, I walked up and invited him to a pie-off my housemates and I were hosting the next day. And he came! He made apple pie, stuck around for the judging (which he won, of course) and then stole away in his little orange VW and left my life forever. I spent months writing my own awful, sappy folk songs about him. A friend of mine saw him play in Austin, Texas, last year, and his songs, my friend says, are just as terrible as they've always been. "Terrible?" I said, shocked. "But he used to be so wonderful!" "No, Thisbe, he was always terrible. You were deafened by love." I've gone back and listened to his tapes, and I'm both horrified and rather pleased to discover that they are absolutely, unquestionably horrendous. Not worse than mine, but pretty damn bad. The apple pie recipe, on the other hand, is still great.

2 frozen pie crusts, thawed
8 large apples, cooking types (*not* Red Delicious!)
Juice of 1 big lemon
Sugar
Cinnamon
Mace
Nutmeg
Unsalted butter
The white of 1 large egg, beaten
    with a bit of water

Preheat the oven to 450°F. Peel, core and slice the apples. Mix them with the lemon juice. Add the sugar and cinnamon to your taste (different apples and different taste buds will necessitate varying amounts of sugar. I'm a fan of a more tart apple pie myself, but you can do what you like). Add a pinch each of mace and nutmeg. Pour the apples into one pie shell, mound toward the center, and dot with butter. Remove the second pie crust from its plate and give it a little roll with the rolling pin so it's of a shape and consistency that you can lay it over the apples and seal up the edges. Cut some slits in the top crust for steam to escape, brush the top with the egg white stuff, and put the pie in the oven on a cookie sheet to catch overflow and drips. After about 10 minutes, turn the heat down to 350 degrees and bake for another hour until the pie is golden brown. If the edges start to get too dark, but the middle isn't as golden as you want, cover the edges with aluminum foil.

DERRICK VANDERNAGLE'S MOTHER'S CHOCOLATE CHIP COOKIES

A picture exists of Derrick Vandernagle and me standing together, naked, in a champagne bucket. We were two. Our mothers were in a food co-op together, and became friends in a warehouse in downtown L.A. at 4:30 A.M. one morning. They were loading crates of eggs into our station wagon when Lucy, his mother, who was four months pregnant, miscarried. My mother helped and comforted her, and they were inseparable until Lucy abruptly left her husband and moved to Maine with Derrick. We received two letters containing little but descriptions of the landscape and thinly veiled hints that Lucy had realized she was a lesbian.

I haven't the slightest idea where Derrick Vandernagle is now, and the only reminder I have, besides that picture (which I can't find), is the recipe for chocolate chip cookies his mother gave my mother, so many years ago. I have finally mastered the recipe (making perfect chocolate chip cookies is so much harder than it would seem), and if I ever meet him I will make these for him and try to glean some more information about his mysterious mother, and her role in his equally mysterious life.

1 $1/2$ cups brown sugar

2 sticks unsalted butter (8 ounces), at room temperature

1 teaspoon vanilla extract

1 teaspoon salt

2 eggs

2 cups whole-wheat flour

1 teaspoon baking powder

1 bag semisweet chocolate chips or chocolate chunks

Preheat the oven to 375°F. Cream the brown sugar and butter at slow speed for 2 minutes. Add the vanilla, salt and eggs. Mix the ingredients for 1 minute at slow speed, then 2 minutes on high. Add the flour and baking powder until the dough is smooth. Add the chocolate chips, then mix for 1 minute on low speed. (If you haven't guessed, you need a mixer for this recipe, or else a lot of patience and very strong arms.) Drop tablespoons of the dough onto ungreased cookie sheets and bake for 10 minutes. The cookies will be soft and gooey inside, but crispy on the outside. Remove sheets from oven and transfer cookies to a wire cooling rack.

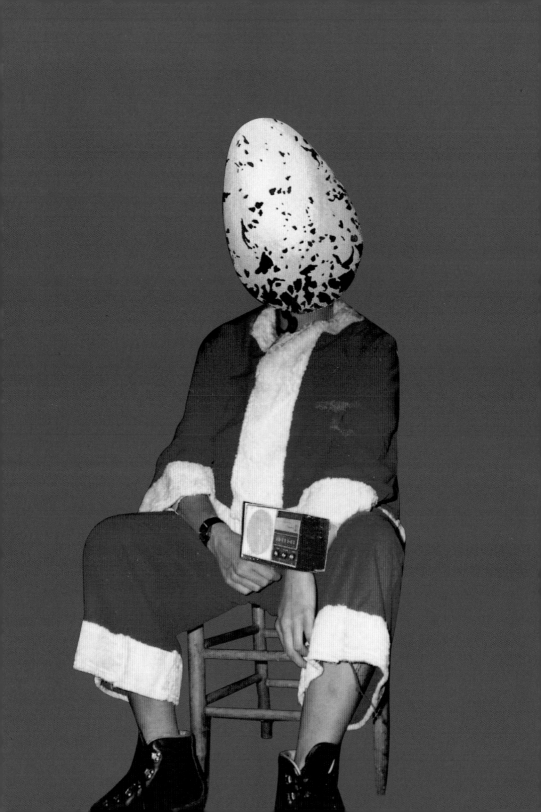

Jim Mossberger's Morning-After Coffee Cake

Wimpy Eddie Plinkett's Manly Quiche

Henry's Buckwheat Pancakes

Wesley Kresbaugh's Cottage Cheese Pancakes

Stan the Postman's Zucchini Bread

Ralph's Popcorn Cake

Sort of Fluffy Things

Backcountry Bread Baking with Chef Morgan

Paul Sorrensen's Crab Quiche

The Masked Bandit's Banana Chocolate Chip Cake

Jared's Holiday French Toast

Lyle's Aunt's Lemon Lush

Ernie the Pilot's Carrot Cake

Arrogant Neil's Stolen Lemon Custard

Jim Mossberger's Morning-After Coffee Cake

I never actually dated Jim Mossberger, but he lived in my apartment complex for six months, and during that time he entertained an astounding number of tall, beautiful women. Actually, now that I think of it, they weren't all tall and beautiful—in fact, he was rather indiscriminate. Perhaps I am simply a lookist and only remember the beautiful ones. In any case, from my kitchen, I could see his front door and also into *his* kitchen. I admit I paid rather close attention, but it was mostly because the women always looked so satisfied and happy and sort of dreamy when they left, and it seemed (honestly) to have something to do with what he served for breakfast. I *needed* that recipe.

So one afternoon I pretended my phone wasn't working and asked to use his, then got him to drink too much Jack Daniel's. It wasn't too hard to get what I'd come for.

1 cup butter
2 cups granulated sugar
2 cups flour
1 teaspoon salt
3 eggs
1 teaspoon vanilla extract
8 ounces sour cream

Filling
1 cup pecans, chopped
2 teaspoons cinnamon
3 tablespoons brown sugar

Preheat the oven to 325°F. Cream the butter and sugar. Sift in the dry ingredients, alternating with the eggs. Mix the batter thoroughly at slow speed, then add the vanilla and sour cream. Pour half of the batter into a well-greased bundt pan (you probably have one in a cupboard somewhere and don't even know it), then add half of the filling, then the rest of the batter. Top with the remaining filling, bake for 65 to 70 minutes and get ready for your luck to change.

Top with brown sugar and nuts. Bake at 325° for 45 minutes. Top with whipped cream and a marshino cherry.

WIMPY EDDIE PLINKETT'S
MANLY QUICHE

Rarely do I think about whether someone is a "real man" or not—I mean, what does that *mean*, anyway? Still, if you're in a Plaid Pantry parking lot in a bad section of Portland, and a strange guy in an overstuffed parka lets himself into the backseat of your car, you want your date to act tough. But Eddie panicked and ran back into the store, leaving me to deal with the situation, which turned out not to be dangerous, just sad. The man, Thomas, told me about his travels in South America, and how he'd returned to find his wife had had a sex change. Somehow, dating a wimpy guy no longer seemed a tragedy.

But anyway, who doesn't eat quiche?

8 slices bacon, crispy fried and crumbled
1 cup shredded Swiss cheese
1 unbaked 9-inch pastry shell
4 eggs, beaten
1 cup sour cream
1 cup half-and-half
2 tablespoons sliced scallions
1 tablespoon flour
Scant teaspoon salt
Pepper, to taste
Dash of cayenne

Preheat the oven to 375°F. Sprinkle the bacon and cheese over the bottom of the pastry shell. In a medium mixing bowl, combine the remaining ingredients and carefully pour over the cheese and bacon. Bake for 25 to 30 minutes until the custard is set and the surface is a very light brown. Let stand 15 minutes before cutting.

HENRY'S BUCKWHEAT PANCAKES

Henry's parents went away for a weekend when we were juniors in high school, and left Henry in change of his little sister Zelda. Henry, in turn, farmed Zelda out to a friend's house and invited me over instead. Ready for a romantic weekend, Henry purchased a box of anticipatory devirginizing condoms, and got a guy we knew with a fake ID to buy two bottles of wine. Then Henry, who at the time was obsessed with the Vietnam War, rented a slew of movies—depressing, wrenching, grueling emotional ordeals over which I expect he wanted to comfort me, segueing into a posttraumatic-movie seduction. Halfway through *Born on the Fourth of July* the phone rang. It was Zelda; she was crying. She and her friend had watched *The Wizard of Oz* and the winged monkeys at the witch's castle had terrified her, and now she couldn't sleep. The upshot was, she wanted to come home. So Henry and I got dressed and went downtown to collect poor Zelly. I wound up sleeping in her room instead of Henry's that night. In the morning, Henry surprised us with pancakes, and Zelly got hers in special shapes—we're talking butterflies, Santa Clauses, her name in pancakes. . . . Henry was very talented with a measuring spoon and a spatula. Why he went into engineering is still a mystery and a sadness to me.

1 cup oats
$^1/_2$ cup buckwheat flour
1 teaspoon baking powder
$1^1/_2$ cups water
2 tablespoons canola oil
1 tablespoon honey

Blend or food-process the oats until you've got oat flour. Blend with the buckwheat flour and baking powder. Grease and heat a skillet. Add wet ingredients to the blender, and blend thoroughly. Pour the batter into the skillet $^1/_4$ cup at a time. Funny shapes optional.

WESLEY KRESBAUGH'S COTTAGE CHEESE PANCAKES

Wesley Kresbaugh and I met while picking apples at Petersons' farm, ten miles outside of Iowa City. He was there because the Petersons were family friends. I was there because I'd responded to an ad in the paper saying they needed help harvesting. I thought it sounded interesting, and, ever on the lookout for a soul mate, I thought maybe there would be a boy picking apples and the boy would be just like me and we would love each other.

About an hour into picking, I was thinking about something besides apples and fell off my ladder. I suspected I had broken my ankle, but there was no one around so I lay on the ground, gathering strength to hop back to the barn. And then, suddenly, standing above me was a very handsome man with long eyelashes and very red, slightly chapped, beautiful lips.

Wesley Kresbaugh was twenty-three and in dental school. There seemed to be an unwritten rule that all young dentists be married and conservative, and Wesley was afraid he was running out of time. So, on the morning of our three-week anniversary, he made these amazing cottage cheese pancakes and said he had something important to ask me. I never suspected (who would?) that he'd put a diamond ring in the batter, and he waited until I nearly broke a tooth to announce that he wanted to spend his life with me. He said *no* was not an answer he would accept. Things went pretty much downhill from there, but I did get the recipe before leaving the state.

3 eggs
1 cup cottage cheese
2 tablespoons oil
1/4 cup flour
1/4 teaspoon salt

Whirl the eggs in a food processor; add the cottage cheese, and whirl again. Add the remaining ingredients and give it one final whirl. Whee!

Cook on a heated griddle or pan and serve with preserves or syrup.

Herbert Hoover's Hometown

THE UNIVERSITY OF IOWA

STAN THE POSTMAN'S ZUCCHINI BREAD

My junior year of college I lived with two wonderful, talented women, and things went swimmingly until Lily's high school boyfriend came to visit. George was very smart and slightly crazy, and was still in love with Lily although she had moved on. But they had stayed friends to an odd, subjective degree, and he called long-distance, weekly, to talk to her.

George was in massage school, although he didn't plan to finish, and we immediately liked each other. At that time, Lily was dating a ridiculous acting student named Friar and had asked me to baby-sit George.

My high school youth pastor had warned that backrubs led to sex and we'd all laughed, disbelieving. But suddenly, there I was, living proof of his proclamation.

Chaos followed. Lily found out and was furious and hurt. George was banned from our apartment; I was called all sorts of derogatory things and expected to move out. Lily told the whole story to another high school friend, Charlie in La Jolla, and three days before I moved, the buzzer rang downstairs. The postman was on the steps, an underpostaged letter in his hand. "Are you Lily Bruner?" he asked.

"No, I'm her roommate," I said.

He blushed and coughed, and I looked at the letter in my hand. Underneath the name Lily Bruner, in block letters, was I CAN'T BELIEVE HE ACTUALLY FUCKED YOUR ROOMMATE.

The postman and I became friends because of this strange encounter, and the next day he invited me over for dinner. We were far too different ever to be compatible romantically, but to follow our meal of Chinese takeout, he'd made this heavenly zucchini bread. I didn't think I even liked zucchini bread, but Stan changed my mind.

3 eggs
1 cup oil
2 cups sugar
3 cups flour
2 cups grated zucchini
3 teaspoons vanilla extract
1 teaspoon salt
1 teaspoon baking soda
3 teaspoons cinnamon
$1/4$ teaspoon baking powder
$3/4$ teaspoon nutmeg
Scant $3/4$ teaspoon cloves

Preheat the oven to 325°F.

Beat the eggs until foamy, then mix the oil and sugar, then add the zucchini and vanilla. Sift the dry ingredients, then combine the wet and dry ingredients, and pour into two loaf pans. Bake for 1 hour.

RALPH'S POPCORN CAKE

Maybe this recipe is a little white-trashy, but if you grew up in a household of health fanatics who never ate white sugar, and then a nice boy named Ralph makes you this better-than-anything cake, you will love him for life. You won't really, but you'll say it, and then spend the next two months trying to extricate yourself from a relationship that was suddenly not what you thought it was. Oops.

1 cup butter or margarine
1 small bag marshmallows
4 cups popped corn
1 cup M&Ms
1 cup gumdrops
1 cup salted peanuts

Melt the butter and add the marshmallows, stirring until melted. Pour over the popcorn and stir in the candy and nuts. Press into a tube pan, like for angel food cake. Let stand and harden, then cut with sharp knife.

41

BACKCOUNTRY BREAD BAKING
WITH CHEF MORGAN

Once, while camping with some friends in a mountain range whose location I've promised to keep secret so as to preserve its unspoiled beauty from tourist hordes, I met Morgan, a lone hiker who passed our campsite and stopped for a few hours to talk and share our fire. By the light of the flames he wrote out for me his backcountry bread recipe on the blank side of a "How to Be a Minimum Impact Hiker" handout. Little did I know that bread could be "baked" over an open fire. Sometimes I wonder if it ever happened at all.

Mix and let sit

$1^1/2$ cups lukewarm water

$1/2$ tablespoon yeast (more in colder weather—yeast is happiest at 105°–110°F)

$1/2$ teaspoon salt

1 tablespoon sugar

1 tablespoon oil

Gradually add about $3^1/2$ cups flour (amount can vary a lot; half white, half wheat flour is best). Stir a lot! No lumps! As you stir, gluten will begin to form (which means the flour mixture will start looking stringy. Gluten is a protein reaction, and lots of stringy gluten is a good thing. You want a good strong gluten).

Knead for about 10 minutes (you want it smooth, not sticking to your hands, which means you should be adding flour as you need/knead it).

Let rise. When it's pouffed up over the top of your bowl, punch it back down (literally, but don't hurt yourself).

Lay the dough into a greased and floured pan (probably the fry-pan of your cook set, it needs to be one that has a lid). Let the dough rise again.

Meanwhile, get a nice fire going, get some bigger pieces of wood on and let it burn down, so that you've got good heat but not big flames. Cover with a grate and place pan on the *edge* of the grate so it's not directly over the fire but still getting heat off it. Grease the inside lid of the pan and place it over the dough. Now you're ready to build what Morgan called a "twiggy fire": a small fire made of tiny twigs that you build *on top of* the lid of the pan (see, you're cooking the bread from the top and the bottom, sort of like in an oven). Now you've got the pan on the edge of the grate, and you want to cook it in fourths, meaning you'll rotate the pan four times during the cooking process (every 5 minutes). Use a small stone placed on the pan lid to mark the first quarter that sits closest to the fire, just so you don't forget where you started. In about 20 minutes, you should have BREAD!

Note: don't be upset if you've got some burned patches or some doughy patches. Think about it this way: you just made fresh bread, without an oven, in the middle of the woods; you think anyone's going to have the gall to complain about a little charcoal?

Paul Sorrensen's Crab Quiche

Paul is the son of friends of my folks whom I met one summer on Cape Cod. We were invited over to the Sorrensens' for lunch, and Paul had made the quiche himself (the recipe for which my mother extracted from Mrs. Sorrensen). I tasted it and fell instantly and doe-eyed into crush. After lunch, we hula-hooped together in the backyard until I started to feel nauseated. When we were leaving, he kissed me good-bye on the cheek, and told my parents that he was falling madly in love with me and they'd better call him when I was ready to get married. I cried in the car on the way home. He was nineteen. I was six.

4 eggs
1 cup sour cream
1 cup small-curd cottage cheese
3/4 cup grated Parmesan cheese
1/4 cup flour
Pinch of salt
4 drops Tabasco
Pinch of nutmeg
3/4 cup diced crabmeat
2 cups shredded Monterey Jack cheese

Preheat the oven to 350°F.

Butter a pie plate.

In the food processor, blend the eggs, sour cream, cottage cheese, Parmesan cheese, flour, salt, Tabasco and nutmeg.

Pour into a large bowl. Stir in the crabmeat and Jack cheese.

Pour into the prepared pie plate.

Bake 40 to 60 minutes until the quiche is solid and the top is golden brown.

THE MASKED BANDIT'S BANANA CHOCOLATE CHIP CAKE

My senior year in college I lived with eight women in a huge yellow house known on campus for decades as "Banana House." In a small college town surrounded by cornfields, there wasn't a whole lot going on, so people got pretty inventive when it came to throwing parties. I remember lots of theme stuff: kissing parties, whore parties (which actually involved the distribution of play money with which you'd have to go around and proposition people . . . but that's a whole other story), drag balls, costume extravaganzas, black-tie-only parties, naked parties . . . you name it. So, the year that we lived in Banana House, we took up the call and held a few parties of our own. One of the best was on Halloween. We hung up signs all over campus, had two different jazz bands play in our living room, and didn't let anyone in the door unless they came bearing some banana-related offering. We got a lot of bizarre gifts that night, some of which are probably unmentionable, but one of the best was this chocolate chip banana bread brought to us by a guy dressed in a cape-and-mask ensemble. And it was I, later in the evening, who undressed him out of it. He borrowed a pair of jeans and a sweatshirt to go home the next day, leaving his baking pan as collateral in the deal. When he brought

halloween party scene! banana house
silly mouse Saturday night fright! de
light! beer here don't fear plenty o'kegs
arms and legs bands hands wonderland(s)
all at 30 Groveland (s) games flames phony
names two dollars dog collars apple bobbin'
cradle robbing be bums bring —
your chum ats i lots of sweets
treats oh my god we having
tos... doesn't rhyme Never mind.

back my clothes (washed and folded),
this recipe was tucked in the pocket of my
jeans. Why I did not marry this man on
the spot is entirely unclear.

> 1 cup sugar
> $1/2$ cup butter
> 1 egg
> 3 frozen mashed bananas
> 3 tablespoons cream
> 2 cups flour
> 1 teaspoon baking powder
> $1/2$ teaspoon baking soda
> 1 cup chocolate chips
> (you can add walnuts if you like, but I don't)

Preheat the oven to 350°F. Blend the sugar, butter and egg. Whip
it all up nice and fluffylike. In another bowl, mash up the bananas
with the cream. In a third bowl (a big one this time), mix the flour
and the baking powder/soda. To this mixture alternately add the but-
ter/sugar mixture and the banana mush until they're all in there, but
DO NOT OVERMIX. We put this in capital letters because it is
important. Otherwise, you'll wind up with a big old brick of a cake
instead of the delightfully fluffy and airy one that my masked bandit
intended. Stir in chips, pour into a greased loaf pan and bake for 50
minutes to an hour. Do the toothpick test. Don't overbake it. Let it
cool before you try taking it out of the pan, okay?

JARED'S HOLIDAY FRENCH TOAST

Jared was working as a Santa in the Meier and Frank where I was getting paid $6 an hour to spray perfume on cards and hand them to people as they entered. Considering that my teaching position at a community college paid about the same, I thought it a rather lucrative form of amusement.

Jared liked being Santa. A lot. He'd gone through the five-hour training seminar offered through human resources meant to keep the Santas from being arrested and to help them understand just what they could and couldn't do. Advised to use their best judgment, they did role-playing to help them deal with difficult situations that might arise.

At the end of his three weeks as Santa, Jared had earned $1,100 (a large portion of which were tips), twenty-four notes from mothers who hoped for a nighttime visit, and several large bruises from kids who were convinced (rightly) that he was a fraud. He kept the beard and hat, and I saw more than I wanted to of both items in the next few months that we dated.

I've been known to take things too far, but it got a little ridiculous. How many times can you be asked to sit on Santa's lap and tell him what you want for Christmas? Actually, I know the answer to that seemingly rhetorical question—eight. Definitely no more than eight.

Because of the Rudolph the Red-Nosed Reindeer movie where Mrs. Claus is concerned about Santa being plump enough, and repeatedly says, "Eat, Santa, eat!" Jared ate a lot of high-calorie comfort food during his Santa days. And this was his favorite breakfast:

3 eggs
3/4 cup milk
1 tablespoon granulated sugar
1/4 teaspoon vanilla extract
1/8 teaspoon salt
8 slices thick bread
Confectioners' sugar (for garnish)

Heat a well-greased griddle to 375°F or a skillet to medium-low. Beat the eggs, milk, granulated sugar, vanilla and salt until smooth. Dip the bread into the mixture and place on the skillet. Cook about 4 minutes on each side, or until light brown. Sprinkle with confectioners' sugar and serve with butter and warmed maple syrup.

LYLE'S AUNT'S LEMON LUSH

I met Lyle at a mutual friend's wedding in Detroit, and during the reception he made me laugh so hard I spilled my entire glass of Cabernet down the front of my beautiful pale green bridesmaid's dress. He followed me into the women's bathroom and kissed me, hard, then cleaned my dress (or tried to) with his water-dampened tie.

As we danced, Lyle dipped me so deeply that my hair touched the floor. Something about being dipped hard and deep, as with jumping on a trampoline, has always made me laugh, but this was real, from-the-gut laughter, making me believe I was exactly where I was meant to be in this life, at this moment.

Of course, weddings always call things into question, since the copious amounts of wine consumed make the questions incredibly easy to answer. Over the next month Lyle and I wrote impassioned letters to each other about the nature of love and destiny and how fantasy and reality can truly coexist. We were made for each other, no question about it.

He lived in San Francisco and I in Georgia, so we decided to meet halfway, in Des Moines, Iowa. In our room at the Bliss Motel, complete with vibrating bed and smoky curtains, we sat across from each other on the flowered comforter and talked. He was different than I remembered—smaller, less dashing. He was funny, charming, and real. I suppose I didn't realize he would be; in letters he was magical, inventive, *not real*. Our relationship had grown in the literary corridor that hangs over the country, where letters are sent and received and which, finally, do little to show who a person truly is, or who they would be with you. Only who they wish to be, and whom I wished to be. And now I saw that this was like any other relationship, consisting of two people with enormous, unfulfillable expectations who are desperate to feel that they'd figured out what everyone else had always figured out first.

I don't think about him now except if I reread his letters, and then I always think, *How is it that we are strangers to each other now?*

But what a silly thing to let go of, hope.

Step 1: Work together 1 cup flour and 1 stick (4 ounces) butter or margarine. Press into a greased 9 X 13-inch pan and bake at 375°F for 15 minutes.

Step 2: Mix one 8-ounce package cream cheese with 1 cup Cool Whip and 1 cup confectioners' sugar. Spread over the crust.

Step 3: Mix 2 packages instant lemon pudding with 3 cups milk. Pour over Step 2 ingredients. Let set. Top with whipped cream and nuts.

Ernie the Pilot's Carrot Cake

In my life, I have only ever had one encounter in an airplane bathroom. All we did was kiss, and he was a pilot, which somehow enabled me not to feel too sleazy about the whole thing. He was off duty, flying home to Tucson, where I was going to visit a friend. We were seated next to each other for the flight and got to talking. He was fastidiously polite, the most all-American boy you've ever seen, but there was this other side to him that drew me in. He raised Angora rabbits as a hobby and had competed as a horse jumper in his youth. We chatted throughout our pitiful airline meal, noting with particular anguish the square of beige sponge that was trying to pass for carrot cake. Ernie had also, as it turned out, worked for some years as the head baker for a Tucson caterer and promised me he had the definitive carrot cake recipe, which he gave to me. I looked it over and announced that carrot cake was not carrot cake unless it was finished with cream cheese icing. He vehemently disagreed, with a great deal of unforeseeable ire, and by the time we landed we were very glad to quit each other's company. It seemed incomprehensible that just hours before I'd been wedged up against the bathroom soap dispenser— one foot on the toilet, the other braced against the door—and to know that not even such newfound lust can transcend a monumental incompatibility like to ice or not to ice. To this day I stand my ground on the cream cheese frosting issue, but I also must admit that Ernie's carrot cake is nonetheless very good, just as long as you don't think too hard about what's missing.

3/4 cup safflower or canola oil
3/4 cup brown sugar
2 eggs
3/4 cup whole wheat flour
1/4 cup white flour

$1/2$ teaspoon baking powder

$1/4$ teaspoon baking soda

$1/2$ teaspoon salt

1 teaspoon cinnamon

$1 1/2$ cups grated carrots

6 tablespoons raisins and/or chopped
walnuts

Preheat the oven to 350°F. Cream together the oil, brown sugar and eggs. Mix together the flours, baking powder, baking soda and salt. Add the dry ingredients to the wet, and beat well. Add the carrots. Blend well. Add the raisins and/or nuts.

Pour into a greased loaf or tube pan and bake 40 minutes. Do a toothpick test to check for doneness. If you don't know what a toothpick test is, read a real cookbook and then come back to us.

53

ARROGANT NEIL'S STOLEN LEMON CUSTARD

There are things I've lost to relationships that I know will never be recovered. These are not shadowy issues of self-esteem, pain or pride, but specific artifacts that I will always berate myself for not being more careful with.

The things I most regret losing are pictures, two in particular, to one particular boy. The first was one of me as a freshman in high school—I was on the basketball "B" team, which meant I was horrible but had a lot of energy—where I had the ball and a scrunched-up face, fighting off two very tall girls of the opposing team. I gave it to this boy because it was so funny, but said I wanted it back at some point. Of course, I remembered it after things got ugly and that was too late.

The second was a picture taken of me by my first love one afternoon on the Oregon coast, on what was, still, one of the best days of my life. I'm not very photogenic but this picture was lovely, capturing the entirety of my youth and hope and affection. It was the picture I'd hoped to show my eventual grandchildren so they could understand who I had been.

This boy, Neil, kept the pictures, as well as a signed copy of *Housekeeping* (a novel by Marilynne Robinson), and tucked inside was the only known copy of my grandmother's lemon custard! I've tried to convince friends to contact my ex and try to wangle the recipe and book from him, but they refuse. Perhaps he never read the book, and perhaps he doesn't even know the recipe inside is as good as it is. Perhaps he has sold it for cash and the book and recipe are now cherished as they should be, somewhere in South Carolina.

I found another lemon custard recipe that is almost as good as my grandmother's, although nothing will ever match it. I'm sure everyone has had at least one of this sort of tragedy occur and will take a moment, with me, to mourn these sorts of losses. Jesus, what were we thinking?

2 tablespoons butter
7/8 cup sugar
3 eggs, separated
1 cup milk
1 1/2 tablespoons flour
1/3 cup lemon juice
Grated zest of lemon

Preheat the oven to 350°F. Beat the butter until soft, then gradually add the sugar. Beat in the egg yolks one by one. Add the milk, flour, lemon juice and zest—beat to mix well. Beat the egg whites until they form soft peaks, then fold into a baking dish and set the dish in a pan of hot water that comes halfway up the side of the dish. Bake for 50 to 60 minutes. Let cool and serve tepid or chilled. (I think warmish is best.)

Murray Dinkel's Egg Salad

Jesse's Wonder Woman–Inspired Tuna Croquettes

Chip's Ceviche

John's Spinach-Orange Salad

Lucas Amarati's Gazpacho

Josh's Spinach-Strawberry Salad

The Legend of Beet Man

Jesus' Sprouts

Savory Things

Wacked-Out Will's Wonderful Wings

Sullivan's Cold Rice Salad

Bielski the Phallus-Fetishist's Vegetarian Maki

Sonny's Magical Squash Casserole

Dan's Deviled Eggs

Casey's Mom's Best Pasta Salad Ever, or Else

JD's Oriental Chicken Salad

Crazy Hank's Curried Chicken Salad

Area 52 Gravlax

MURRAY DINKEL'S
EGG SALAD

Murray was my boyfriend in kindergarten, which meant that he called me names, tried to trip me in the hallway during fire drills, and threw chunks of egg salad at me from his lunchbox when I refused to kiss him during recess.

$2/3$ cup mayonnaise
2 tablespoons lemon juice
2 teaspoons red wine vinegar
1 tablespoon fresh parsley, minced
$1/4$ cup finely chopped celery
8 hard-boiled eggs, diced
Salt and pepper

Mix the mayo, lemon juice, vinegar and parsley until blended. Add the celery and eggs, and stir. Add salt and pepper to taste. Don't throw your food.

JESSE'S WONDER WOMAN–INSPIRED TUNA CROQUETTES

Jesse had one whole bedroom wall plastered with Wonder Woman paraphernalia, which he had been collecting since he was twelve. He refused to be embarrassed by it, or to concede the possibility that it might hint at the fact that his orientation was not what it seemed.

Jesse was also completely enamored of his mother with whom he lived. He made her breakfast and rubbed her feet and called her pet names: Gunga Din, Peppermint Mom and, most often, the Other Wonder Woman.

Comparing myself daily to hundreds of images of Wonder Woman made me feel small and unremarkable. (Who could compete with Wonder Woman?) The fact that Jesse worshiped an incredibly strong, resourceful, imaginary woman with an invisible jet made it a little easier when he dumped me for a guy named Chip in his pottery class. We always want to think that someone who doesn't recognize our charms is gay, but, well, sometimes it's true. We are still friends, and he is my number one fashion consultant.

As Jesse made this, he recited the recipe in a wobbly nasal voice that was supposed to be his mother's. He actually sounded *exactly* like his mother, and the fact that Jesse was wearing her shiny red bathrobe and shower cap made the performance all the more entertaining and deeply disturbing. I will omit the embellishments that occurred.

Make a very thick white sauce (this makes 2 cups):
Melt 4 tablespoons butter, then add 5 tablespoons all-purpose flour.

Add 1 teaspoon salt and $1/8$ teaspoon pepper. Slowly add 1 cup hot milk, and stir over low heat until thick. Stir in 1 to 2 large cans white-meat albacore tuna and chill the mixture.

Form into croquettes (patties) and roll in beaten egg, and then roll in crushed saltine crackers. Chill for 1 hour.

In a skillet, sauté the croquettes in melted butter until brown, then serve with lemon and/or tartar sauce. Just marvelous, sweetie pie.

CHIP'S CEVICHE

Chip was a fisherman on the island where my parents and I spent the summers of my early childhood, and though he was a good forty years my senior, I had a mad crush on him that persisted until he and his wife, Betty, sold their fish market and retired to Florida. Chip was everything a fisherman should be: hulking, grizzled and weatherbeaten, and missing a few teeth. And Betty was an absolute tart: sassy and mean, and captain of her women's bowling league. Together, Chip and Betty ran a little lunch counter alongside the fish market, where they served up the day's catch amid burbling lobster tanks and swooping old fishnets festooned with cracked plastic buoys and flashing Christmas lights. It was a child's dream! And while most of the children who came to dine at the fish market opted for the standard popcorn shrimp and fried fish sticks, I—in what I am sure was an attempt to gain the favor and admiration of Chip and to distinguish myself from the rest of the kid-rabble—was a die-hard fan of the ceviche. Now, there's ceviche and there's ceviche, but there is no ceviche like Chip's ceviche, and that will be enormously clear when you taste it.

> 1 pound scallops (if they're bay, leave 'em whole; if they're sea,
>   cut 'em into fourths)
> Juice of 5 to 6 limes, enough to cover the scallops
> 2 tablespoons finely chopped garlic
> 2 tablespoons finely chopped parsley
> About 3 tablespoons olive oil
> Salt and freshly ground black pepper

Marinate the scallops in the lime juice for at least 4 hours in the fridge. Drain, and add the garlic, parsley, olive oil, and salt and pepper to taste. Serve over a bed of lettuce.

JOHN'S SPINACH-ORANGE SALAD

I met John in an otherwise empty Laundromat on a Saturday night, and I immediately assumed that he was, like me, a graduate student (who else would be doing their laundry on such an important night?). Halfway through grading his large stack of papers and more than halfway through the beer he'd brought, he asked for help finishing both. By the time we finished the beer and went for more, I'd decided he was exactly the person I'd been dying to meet. He wanted to make me dinner the following night, and I drove home, giddy, thinking, *Finally! A worthy man!*

John was studying art history, although he had said his real love was black-and-white photography, so I was rather surprised to find his apartment walls plastered with magazine images of women, most in scanty attire. Above each, he'd attached a paper dialogue bubble which said things like, "John, you're such a *stud*," and "John, do that *again*, but harder." Marilyn Monroe's bubble said, "I'm so hungry I could eat a horse, but John, you're close enough."

The really inexplicable thing is that I stayed for dinner and let him take my picture (clothed! clothed!). We then got into a nasty fight about the validity of *The Beauty Myth* by Naomi Wolf, and I threw my glass of wine in his face. I shudder to think what *my* dialogue bubble said.

$1/2$ cup vegetable oil
$1/4$ cup slivered almonds
$1/4$ cup red wine vinegar
1 teaspoon sugar
$1/2$ teaspoon salt
$1/4$ teaspoon pepper
3 oranges, peeled and
    sliced crosswise
$1/2$ red onion, thinly sliced
4 cups torn spinach leaves,
    large stems removed

Heat the oil over moderate heat. Add the slivered almonds and cook until golden, stirring, for 2 to 4 minutes. Remove the skillet from the fire.

Transfer the almonds to a small bowl with a slotted spoon. For the dressing, add the vinegar, sugar, salt and pepper to the oil, stirring until the sugar dissolves. Set aside. In a large bowl, combine the oranges, onion and spinach leaves. Sprinkle with the almonds; pour the dressing over and toss until the spinach is well coated. Serves four. Or one, if you're hungry enough to eat a horse.

LUCAS AMARATI'S GAZPACHO

Lucas was my boyfriend the first of two summers I worked on an organic vegetable farm in Virginia. He was a beautiful, impish, little long-haired hippie boy, and the sight of him, shirtless, hefting hay bales from the back of a pickup truck, his army shorts hanging low off his hips, never failed to make my knees go weak. We grew a lot of vegetables on the farm, but mostly an extraordinary number of tomatoes. Twenty-seven varieties that summer: Pink Girls, Better Boys, Brandywine, Pruden's Purple. . . Our compost piles were tremendous mounds of tomatoes in every shade from lemon to deep eggplant. We were allowed to use as much produce as we wanted for personal consumption, so in order to feed ourselves cheaply, we perfected a number of tomato recipes. My absolute favorite Virginia tomato dish was Lucas's gazpacho. It's honestly out of this world. The fact that I have this recipe almost makes up for the fact that when he left at the end of the summer to travel in Nepal, I only got one postcard and then never heard from him again.

1 garlic clove
3 to 4 ripe tomatoes, quartered
$^1/_2$ green pepper, cut into chunks
$^1/_2$ small onion, cut into chunks
1 cucumber, peeled and cut into chunks
1 teaspoon salt
$^1/_4$ teaspoon pepper
2 tablespoons olive oil
3 tablespoons red wine vinegar
$^1/_2$ cup ice water

Blend all the ingredients a very short time. Do not pulverize; leave some chunks of vegetables. Refrigerate before serving.

JOSH'S SPINACH-STRAWBERRY SALAD

For a *very* short time I hung out with John's (see John's Spinach-Orange Salad four pages back) twin brother, Josh, and I had to stifle my amazed laughter when one night he prepared a salad that seemed a direct descendant of John's. Both (salads) are excellent, so although they're similar, I wanted to give you a choice. It's always good to have a choice, even if it is between machismo and egocentricity.

1 pound fresh spinach, washed and stemmed
1 quart strawberries, washed and hulled
$1/3$ cup sugar
$1 1/2$ teaspoons minced red onion
$1/4$ teaspoon Worcestershire sauce
$1/4$ cup apple cider vinegar

$^1/_2$ cup olive oil
2 tablespoons sesame seeds
1 tablespoon poppy seeds
Salt and pepper
$^1/_4$ teaspoon paprika

Chill the spinach and strawberries. For the dressing, mix the sugar, onion, Worcestershire sauce and vinegar in the blender. With the blender running, slowly add the oil. Stir in the sesame and poppy seeds and salt and pepper to taste. Transfer the dressing to a jar with a tight lid, chill and shake well. Put berries and spinach in a big bowl. Toss well with dressing and sprinkle paprika on top. Serves eight.

Hey E.!

stopped by

n is here)

no "E."

THE LEGEND OF BEET MAN

That first summer I worked on the Virginia farm, the summer of Lucas Amarati . . . well, after Lucas left for Nepal, I got kind of bummed out and rebellious and mad that he'd left me, and so on and so on. . . . So I sort of made friends with this other guy on the farm. He was older, and lived in an ancient trailer on the farm property. He worked intermittently and was a basket weaver during the off-season. I spent the rest of the summer hanging out on the ratty couch at his trailer. He was a basic cook, fed himself pretty much solely off the farm produce. And he had a special fondness, bordering on an out-and-out obsession, for beets. Me, I've always liked beets, but once I'd feasted with the Beet Man there was no turning back. Simple is best when it comes to beets, and if you can pull them right out of the ground just before you cook them, well, all the better. If you've only eaten canned beets, you don't even know what a beet is. Make them like this, like the Beet Man did. Then you'll see.

Cut off the beet tops and put the beets in a pot with enough water to cover them fully. Boil for 30 to 40 minutes, or until the beets are tender when stuck with a fork. Drain and rinse in cold water. Remove the skins (do this under running water if the beets are too hot to touch, which they will be). Slice or cut up the beets however you like (although I like them best sectioned in wedges like an orange), and arrange in a shallow bowl. Sprinkle on some coarse kosher salt and grind black pepper, all to your taste. Pour balsamic vinegar and extra virgin olive oil over the beets (enough so that they're sitting in about a quarter-inch of dressing). Serve warm. I'm salivating just writing this recipe down. They're out of this world. Honestly. You will want to live in a rusty trailer and sleep on a ratty couch with the Beet Man for the rest of your life. I swear.

GOOD GUY A·GO·GO

LOOK FOR THE SIGNIFICANCE OF EACH EXPERIENCE.

Jesus' Sprouts

I lived in California for a time and became vaguely obsessed with a guy who worked at the coffeehouse where I hung out. He was beautiful, in a Jesus-y sort of way, and always looked at me as if I possessed some profound knowledge that he was trying to will out through my eyes. I dug that. One weekend he invited me to go backpacking with him down in Death Valley and I accepted, thrilled by a fantasy of cooking together over a fire and cuddling in our sleeping bags at night.

But Jesus' idea of the trip was a little different from mine. He spent three days tripping on mushrooms, during which time he ate nothing but sprouts that he grew himself in a plastic jar with a piece of cheesecloth and a rubber band. He turned out to be an insufferable talker, a pig-headed windbag, and the worst possible product of Robert Bly's men's movement. He acted as if he were the epitome of the evolved and enlightened man when he was really only a New Age–spouting chauvinistic pig. At the risk of incredulity, I will tell you that these words actually issued from his lips: "I think of myself as a consort to the goddess."

When we got home, I switched coffee shops.

Any fresh seed or bean is sproutable. My favorites are alfalfa seeds, mung beans and garbanzo beans, but you can use brown rice, lentils, soybeans, sesame seeds, black-eyed peas, or anything else that suits your fancy. Put the seeds in a clean jar and cover the mouth of the jar with a piece of cheesecloth. Secure with a rubber band. Pour enough water to cover the beans, let it sit a few minutes, then pour out the water. Store the jar in a dark place and repeat the water rinse once a day. The smallest seeds should begin to sprout in about four days; larger ones might take longer. They're great for long backpacking trips when you can't carry fresh vegetables.

WACKED-OUT WILL'S WONDERFUL WINGS

Will was not a stable man. I actually met him (and got this recipe) not long before he voluntarily committed himself to a mental health facility. He checked himself out soon thereafter, realizing, as he put it, that "a loony bin is not a place for people who want to *stop* being loony." He didn't regret his time spent there: he said it made him understand the difference between sanity and insanity, and that was apparently very comforting to him. We did not continue to be involved romantically when he got out of the hospital, though this was not my choice. I kind of adored him. But Will was a sometime-psychic (or so he sometimes believed), and he knew in his heart and in the cards that we were not meant for one another. I think he meant it as something of a consolation prize when, in our final correspondence, before moving to an ashram in New Hampshire, he sent me this horoscope. There was nothing else in the envelope, just the newspaper clipping. I took it to mean: *See, Thisbe, look what you're in for—* "With a little concentration, you can probably have orgasms in your elbows and feet. . . ." *So what do you need with crazy old me?*

CHICKEN

penly being observed the nude?
frequently
occasionally
rarely
ever

fantasies of bei

3 tablespoons soy sauce
3 tablespoons wine vinegar
1/4 cup vegetable oil
1/2 cup brown sugar
1 teaspoon fresh minced ginger
1 garlic clove, minced
3 pounds chicken wings (split the wings and
   discard the tips)

Combine all the ingredients in a shallow dish,
add the chicken wings, and marinate for at least 8
hours or overnight. Bake at 400°F for 45 to 50
minutes, turning once or twice, until brown and
crispy.

SULLIVAN'S COLD RICE SALAD

(OR WHAT WE ATE AFTER MYRTLE BIRNBAUM'S FUNERAL)

Sullivan's grandmother and my grandmother lived in the same seniors' apartment complex in Yonkers, and we saw each other almost every weekend of the first eighteen years of our lives. Our grandmothers played Scrabble together every Sunday afternoon, along with another woman from down the hall named Myrtle Birmbaum. Myrtle's grandson Dougie always wanted to play with me and Sullivan. When Myrtle died a few years ago, Sullivan, Doug and I were reunited at her funeral. We went back to the Birnbaums' to sit shiva, and as is the custom, we brought foods for the buffet table, I a platter of chicken wings (see Wacked-Out Will's Wonderful Wings two pages back), Sullivan this exquisite rice salad. The dishes complemented one another, and I now serve them as an ensemble. Sometimes I think it's too bad that Sullivan and I never had any romantic feelings for one another, because we could've gone nicely together I think, like rice salad and chicken wings.

2 cups cooked rice, cold (cook it ahead of time and let it
   cool completely; hot or warm rice results in a gloppy,
   gross mess)
4 scallions, chopped
2 navel oranges, cut into bite-size chunks
$1/2$ cup water chestnuts, rinsed

$^1/_3$ cup slivered almonds, toasted (brown them in
   the toaster for 2 to 3 minutes. Watch them
   carefully; as they burn easily and nuts aren't
   cheap)
1 tablespoon soy sauce
2 tablespoons wine vinegar
$^1/_4$ cup oil
Pepper
1 tablespoon minced fresh parsley
$^1/_4$ teaspoon sugar
$^1/_8$ teaspoon dry mustard

Mix together the rice, scallions, oranges, water
chestnuts and almonds. Mix the remaining ingredients together.
   Pour the dressing over the rice mixture and toss to
distribute evenly.

Bielski the Phallus-Fetishist's Vegetarian Maki

Bielski moved to Japan not long after we met, but we corresponded for a time until I realized he was completely off his rocker. We had hooked up and spent a couple nights together during his last month in the U.S., and it had been nice, not earth-shattering, but nice. When he got to Japan he must have been really lonely. Every single day he wrote me a postcard, each picture more phallic than the previous one. It started to get kind of weird. Then it started to get really weird. Then it was seriously weird and I stopped writing back. It took about four months, but finally so did he. Which means I have a hell of a lot of penis postcards in my memorabilia file. Sausages, bratwursts, hot dogs . . . what's odd is he was a vegetarian.

> 1 cup sushi rice or short-
>   grain white rice
> 2 tablespoons rice vinegar
> 1 teaspoon sugar
> 1 teaspoon dry sherry
> 1/2 teaspoon salt
> 1 package nori
> Wasabi, available in tubes

Whatever you like of the following: thinly sliced avocado; peeled and seeded cucumber cut into the thinnest, longest, most stringlike strips possible; carrots and pickled daikon sliced the same way; steamed asparagus, sautéed shiitake mushrooms, scallions, and any other brilliant vegetables that strike your fancy.

Note: this whole thing is decidedly easier if you have a little bamboo mat for rolling, but it's do-able without one.

In a strainer, rinse the rice under cold water until the runoff is clear. In a saucepan bring the rice to a boil with 1 1/4 cups water. Keep it covered and let it simmer for 15 minutes, or until the water is all absorbed and the rice isn't crunchy. (While the rice is cooking, slice up your veggies.) When the rice is done, remove it from the heat and let it stand for 10 more minutes, still covered, then transfer to a large flat pan and spread it out in an even layer. Keep it covered.

In another saucepan, combine the vinegar, sugar, sherry and salt, and heat until the sugar dissolves. Let it cool, and then sprinkle it over the rice.

Lay a piece of the nori on a clean, flat surface. Spread the thinnest possible layer of rice over it, leaving a 1-inch margin on the lengthwise ends. About an inch in from that, use your thumb to press out a depression across the rice. Stroke a bit of wasabi in the depression if you like. That's where you'll lay the veggies. Don't use too many or it'll get hairy later on. Then, with or without a bamboo mat, begin to roll from the vegetable-valley end. When you reach the other end, wet down the unriced margin with a little vinegar or soy on the tip of your finger and seal the roll. Set aside, seam down, until you're ready to slice.

Slicing is best done ice-cream-cake fashion with a big, sharp knife and a tall glass of very hot water in which to dip the knife between slices. You may have to change the water a few times. A towel for wiping off the knife might help too. Cut into 1-inch segments and serve with wasabi and soy sauce for dipping.

SONNY'S MAGICAL SQUASH CASSEROLE

Fifteen miles north of Iowa City is a beautiful old wooden bridge, which I have been taken to twice but never been able to find on my own. Sometimes I see it, looming reddish in the late light, as a sort of Brigadoon, a place that doesn't truly exist in real time.

I wasn't the first (or last) woman Sonny took there, but I daresay I am the only woman who, while eating the marvelous squash casserole he brought, somehow managed to drop both her fork and her shoe into the waters of the Cedar River, thirty feet below. I used to wonder about those single shoes you sometimes see on the edges of roads. Well, I still wonder, although now I understand how those things happen.

1 pound zucchini, cut in chunks
1 small onion, grated
4 eggs, lightly beaten
3/4 cup grated Swiss cheese
3/4 cup grated Cheddar cheese
1/2 teaspoon dried oregano
1/2 teaspoon dried basil
Salt and pepper

Preheat the oven to 325°F for 3 to 4 minutes. Steam the zucchini and onion. Drain and mash. Add the eggs, grated cheeses and zucchini, oregano, basil, salt and pepper to taste, and mix lightly. Pour into a lightly greased casserole dish and bake for 35 to 40 minutes.

Dan's Deviled Eggs

I lost my virginity to Dan Williams in his childhood bedroom while his parents slept soundly down the hall. I'd known Dan since we were all of three years old, and though there wasn't a lot of passion between us, there was a lot of trust, which wound up mattering a lot more than passion that first time around. We never really "dated," Dan and I, but there was always something special between us. Our folks are still friends, and I see him every so often at a family gathering, a barbecue, a potluck fund-raiser. To my parents' annual Bastille Day party one year (don't ask, we're a family of odd traditions), Dan brought these fabulous deviled eggs. I'd forgotten all about deviled eggs, hadn't had them since I was a kid at my grandmother's house. Now, thanks to Dan, I make them for lunch all the time—they're so easy! "And," I can just hear Dan tease, "so were you!" Thank you, Dan, for everything.

8 hard-boiled eggs

1/4 cup Miracle Whip (I fully believe that the world is divided into two kinds of people: the Miracle Whippers and the Mayonnaisers. I am a Whipper through and through, and am convinced that it's the Whip that makes this recipe great, but I understand if you're one of *them* and absolutely *have* to make your deviled eggs with mayo. I take consolation only in knowing that mine taste better!)

2 tablespoons Dijon mustard
1 tablespoon red wine vinegar
1/4 teaspoon salt
Freshly ground black pepper
Paprika

Peel and slice the eggs lengthwise. Scoop out the yolks into a separate bowl and combine with the Miracle Whip, mustard, vinegar, salt and pepper. Spoon the mixture back into the whites and sprinkle with paprika. Pretty.

Casey's Mom's Best Pasta Salad Ever, or Else

Casey was our summer next-door neighbor when I was a kid. It's fair to call him an ex-boyfriend, since we bathed together nearly every day when we got home from the beach, which makes him the first boy ever to see me naked. And it was also with Casey and his brother, whom we called Gleep, that I spent my formative doctor-playing

STORE HOURS
9:30 AM
to
8:00 PM
CLOSED SUNDAYS

OPEN DAILY
SUNDAYS
12 NOON

Reward

Closed
Session

TALK
SOFTLY
PLEASE

HOURS
7:00 - 9:00
OPEN 7 DAYS

FOR
SALE

SALE
Reduced.

years. Our mothers often pooled us kids for dinner so they could cook (and drink gin and tonics) together while they fed us. I always insisted that my mother was a better cook than Casey's, and he and Gleep pretty much agreed with me except when it came to Marcia's pasta salad, over which Casey was willing to fight to the death anyone who didn't concede that it was the greatest thing ever on earth in the whole wide world. Since Casey had a BB gun and somewhat of a sadistic streak, I agreed that this was the best pasta salad I had ever tasted in my life.

1 box rigatoni (tricolor is always festive)
$^1/_2$ can kidney beans
$^1/_2$ can garbanzo beans
2 cups fresh green beans
2 medium tomatoes, diced
8 ounces feta cheese, crumbled
1 cucumber, diced
Bottled Italian or Caesar salad dressing, to taste (or use Perfect Vinaigrette by Arlo in Slippery Things, which is better than anything that comes in a bottle anyday, but don't tell Casey, since he'd probably take it as some kind of disrespect to his mom and come hunt me down)

Cook the pasta. Drain and chill.
Add everything.
Toss with as much dressing as you like.

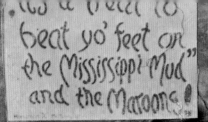
"...is a treat to
beat yo' feet on
the Mississippi Mud"
and the Maroons!"

JD's Oriental Chicken Salad

I met JD at a lesbian potluck, and, as the only nonlesbians at the party, we sort of bonded that night, then dated very casually for a month or so afterward. I cannot for the life of me remember which one of the peace-loving lesbian potluckers brought him along, or why any of them might have been friends with him in the first place. He turned out to be relentlessly egomanical, wildly possessive and somewhat homicidally jealous, with a temper that honestly made me fear for my safety. One evening I had to go to work and I left him hanging out at my apartment. While I was gone, he apparently read a few pages of my journal, which he found stashed under a pile of books by my bed. Enraged by some things I had written (and to this day, I'm not sure what it was that he read that got him so upset), he grabbed a bag of clothes I had been meaning to bring to the dry cleaner, went downstairs to the washing machines and "took care of it for me." He washed and dried everything. In hot water, and on high heat.

Boil a 3-pound chicken. Let it cool in its broth. Remove the meat from the bones and arrange on a bed of greens (watercress is nice).

Mix 4 tablespoons soy sauce, 2 tablespoons honey and 1 clove crushed garlic. Let it sit for 15 minutes or so.

In a saucepan, mix 3 tablespoons peanut or corn oil, 2 finely chopped scallions, 4 slices gingerroot, minced, 1/4 teaspoon red pepper flakes, and a dash of black pepper. Heat this mixture gently for about 5 minutes. Pour it into the soy sauce mixture, and then pour the whole thing over the chicken. Serve at room temperature.

CRAZY HANK'S CURRIED CHICKEN SALAD

For two years I'd seen Hank around campus. He had long, dark hair and a serious expression, like Mr. Darcy would have had if he'd lived in Corvallis, Oregon, rather than in a Jane Austen novel. When Hank went to a coffee shop near campus, he actually went to study, not to look at everyone who came in, hoping to be distracted. As far as I could tell, he did not *get* distracted. Once when we were both in Java Rama, a homeless man named Gary came in screaming at the barista, saying she was part of the capitalist agenda and that he was going to come back with an Uzi and blow her to bits.

Everyone was glancing around nervously, not knowing whether to laugh or hide under their tables, but Hank kept reading. And I didn't talk to him until a year later, when I went to my friend's High Drama Poker Night and he was there. For three weeks, we spent every moment together. In the fourth week, he revealed his obsession with Russian pornography, and a history of abusing small animals.

I moved across the country, though not because of him, exactly. When he decided he was coming with me I did what any conflict-avoider would have done—I cheated on him and told him about it.

Two weeks later, separated by nearly three thousand miles, he called me at three in the morning. "I've been in the university library all week," he said. "I figured out what's wrong with you."

"Wonderful," I said. "What's wrong with me?"

"I'm not going to tell you over the phone," he said. "You've got to meet me somewhere."

"Somewhere where?"

"Just come back. I'll make you some dinner, and I'll tell you."

"Hank, do you know where I am? Do you know what time it is?"

"This is your life I'm talking about! I can help you. I'm the only one who will be honest with you."

"Non est talis rēs et malum puerum"

FORTUNE TELLER

MIRACLE FISH

"So, be honest now."

"Come back," he said.

A few days later, I learned he was going around town, banging on my friends' doors to reveal that I had Histrionic Personality Disorder. I spent a bit of time in the library myself, worried, and during that time he returned a pair of my socks in an envelope with a stamp of Father Flanagan saying, "There are no truly bad boys," in Latin. I guess he forgave me. Last I heard he was married to a Japanese woman and living in Brooklyn. What else can I say? He made a mean curried chicken salad.

3 cups cooked chicken
3/4 cup diced green olives
2 cups sliced celery
2 cups cooked brown rice
1 cup raisins
3/4 cup almonds, chopped
1 cup mayonnaise
2 teaspoons curry powder

Mix. Serve chilled. Fabulous!

Area 52 Gravlax

Look, I can't tell you about the person I got this recipe from. I just can't, okay? Please believe me. It just wouldn't be safe, and I can't go into it. I've said too much already. I could tell you, but then I'd have to kill you.

> 2 pounds center-cut fresh salmon, halved
>   lengthwise
> 1 tablespoon sugar
> 1 tablespoon coarse ground salt
> 1$^1/_3$ tablespoons coarse black pepper
> 1 large bunch dill, coarsely chopped

Remove any small bones with tweezer. Wash and wipe the skin dry. Put the salmon, skin-side down, in a shallow ceramic dish. Combine the sugar, salt and pepper, and sprinkle over the fish. Sprinkle the dill over the salmon. Put the two fish halves together like a sandwich, flesh sides together, in the pan. Place plastic wrap, then aluminum foil on the fish. Place a brick or two cans on top. Keep in the fridge for 3 to 4 days, turning once a day. When ready to serve, scrape the dill from the fish. Slice thinly, garnish with lemon slices. It's incredible with bagels and cream cheese, or just on its own with a good bread. Serve capers or sliced onions alongside if you wish.

The Blackened Red Snapper James Said
He Would Make and Never Did

Poor Donald's Chicken Enchiladas

Lawry's Bloody Marys

Eli's Tossed Spicy Vegetables

Conway's Chiles Rellenos Casserole

Spicy Things

Andre's Parmesan Pesto Dip

Davis's Spicy Southern BBQ Rub

Aaron's Post–Peace Corps Tom Yum Goong

Rhett's Quesadilla Things

Fred Pinto's Taco Soup

Brady's Pepper Cheese Dip

THE BLACKENED RED SNAPPER JAMES SAID HE WOULD MAKE AND NEVER DID

You may wonder if writing the abbreviated versions of all these failed romances can sometimes make you feel sheepish and sad, and the answer is yes. Although you remember the bad things clearly enough, when you close your eyes and imagine the feel of someone's lips on yours, the things he said when he woke up next to you, the last words spoken, you think, *If only this or that had been different, if only . . .*

James is definitely in the *if only* category. He was funny, smart and sexy, and lives two thousand miles away. Distance always seems to

amplify a loss. Perhaps, though, he made me realize there were men out there who were worth crying over, which was necessarily wonderful.

Although he never made this meal that he promised, James did send me the recipe, which turned out to be as perfect as he said it was. He also included a note to make sure I had a powerful fan over my stove or my apartment would be filled with smoke. I didn't and it was but, hey, I recovered. Oh, and this recipe serves eight.

4 teaspoons salt
6 teaspoons paprika
2 teaspoons cayenne pepper
1 1/2 teaspoons white pepper
3/4 teaspoon black pepper
3/4 teaspoon dried thyme
1/2 teaspoon dried oregano
8 skinless red snapper fillets,
    each 8 to 10 ounces
2 sticks (8 ounces) melted butter
8 lemon wedges

Combine all the spices. Make sure the fillets are very cold, and dip both sides of the fish in the spice mixture and make sure all the surfaces are covered well.

Heat a *heavy* skillet over high heat until extremely hot (this is when you want the fan on at high speed). Dip the fish into the melted butter and place directly on the hot skillet. Drizzle with an additional teaspoon of butter, and cook for 2 minutes, then turn. Drizzle with more butter and cook an additional minute. Serve with lemon wedges.

POOR DONALD'S CHICKEN ENCHILADAS

Lord, where do I start? Donald was a friend of an acquaintance and I was going through a bit of a dry spell, so I agreed to go to a movie with him. I arrived at his apartment to find a rather normal-looking man with a sweet, slow smile. Once we got out of the apartment, however, he turned to me and said, "Listen, I'm shrooming, and I need you to hold on to my hand. Don't let go for any reason. Hold on really tight, okay? I mean it."

It's very difficult to do anything when someone won't let go of your hand, but I made it through the taxi hailing and the ticket and popcorn buying, and just decided to keep my coat on and forgo any trips to the bathroom. My hand ached, but when the movie started I made myself forget that I was on a terrible date and focused on the subtitles. Maybe twenty minutes later, poor Donald reached over with his free hand and grabbed at my shoulder. His face was grayish and his eyes were bugged out. "Do you need to go home?" I whispered. He did, desperately.

Back at his apartment, I was (still holding his hand) inching toward the door when he reestablished his grip and pleaded with me not to leave him. "I can't be alone tonight. I really, really can't," he said. He was on the verge of tears, so I agreed to stay, and we went to bed, clothed, still holding hands.

In the middle of the night, I woke to a warm pressure on my stomach. I looked down and gasped. Donald woke up and shouted, "Don't move! Don't move! It's the kittens!"

Donald's cat was giving birth on my midsection. I kid you not. And this weird, miraculous night turned into a relationship of sorts. And then I found out about the voyeurism, the little-girl-lust, and his still-in-the-picture ex-girlfriend, a loud, funny Samoan woman who was a "better person" than me. What can I say? I tried. I did. This recipe was, I suppose, a lovely parting gift.

$^1/_3$ cup water

6 tablespoons oil

$^1/_3$ cup minced onion

2$^1/_2$ tablespoons flour

One 8-ounce can tomato sauce

1 tablespoon chili powder

$^1/_4$ teaspoon dried oregano

$^1/_4$ teaspoon garlic powder

Salt

2 cups cooked chicken, diced

1 cup sour cream

1 cup half-and-half

1$^1/_2$ tablespoons butter

$^1/_2$ cup chicken broth

12 tortillas

1 cup shredded sharp Cheddar cheese

Preheat the oven to 350°F. Heat 3 tablespoons of the oil in a medium saucepan, add the onion and cook 4 minutes (exactly 4, mind you). Add 1 tablespoon of the flour and stir until browned. Add the tomato sauce, water, chili powder, oregano, garlic powder and salt to taste. Simmer, uncovered, for 10 minutes, then add the chicken and sour cream. Mix well and set aside.

Combine the half-and-half and broth in a saucepan and heat. Make a paste with the remaining 1$^1/_2$ tablespoons flour and the same amount of butter. Add the broth mixture and stir until thickened. Dip the tortillas into the mixture, then spoon $^1/_2$ cup of that yummy stuff onto each tortilla, roll and place, seam side down, in a baking dish. Pour the remaining sauce over the enchiladas and sprinkle with cheese. Bake for 20 minutes or broil until cheese is melted. Garnish as desired. Serves six, unless one of those six is really hungry.

Lawry's Bloody Marys

Lawry was one of twenty-seven Thanksgiving guests one year at our Iowa farmhouse. We covered a Ping-Pong table with old quilts for tablecloths, used stacked crates and end tables as extra chairs, and prepared to have twenty-seven people sleeping on the floor of the living room, since the Bloody Marys that Lawry started mixing at about 10:30 in the morning were deceptively strong. My boyfriend at the time (see Smitty's Smoked Turkey in Substantial Things) was outside most of the day proving his manhood by tending the barbecue coals. Inside, Lawry kept our Bloody Mary glasses filled and repeatedly asked me if I wanted to go upstairs and let him suckle my breast. I was apparently both sober enough to mock him relentlessly for being such an unabashed pig, and drunk enough to wind up making out with him in the bathroom while the marshmallow yams caught fire in the oven and I decided no one would notice our absence in all the commotion. When the flames were put out, Lawry and I emerged into a roomful of people who were all well aware that he hadn't been helping me plunge the toilet, as I claimed. It was then brought to my attention that in the course of the day he'd already spent time "plunging the toilet" with Jennifer Massey and Robin Elks. I sobered up quickly.

1 quart tomato juice
Juice of 1 1/2 lemons
A few tablespoons horseradish (to your taste)
A few shakes of Worcestershire sauce (to your taste)
Freshly ground black pepper (guess how much?)

Mix all the ingredients in a pitcher. Fill glasses with ice and as much vodka as you like (i.e., as drunk as you'd like to be). Pour in the tomato mixture and stir well. Cut a lemon into slices for garnish. (I like to rub it on the rim of the glass, give it a little squeeze and drop it in.) Drink at your own discretion.

ELI'S TOSSED SPICY VEGETABLES

On the second shelf of my bathroom cabinet, behind the fifteen-year-old bottle of Jean Naté I can't bear to throw away, is an embarrassing reminder of my failed romance with Eli: a black plastic bag containing two unopened boxes of extra-large condoms.

Perhaps (obviously) I had been too hopeful, too quick to make the trip to Fantasy Video, the only place one can buy extra-large condoms. Eli and I had only had sex twice, but had broken both condoms, so I didn't want to wait around.

Even being in a porn shop was horribly embarrassing for me, and asking for extra-large condoms took all the chutzpah I could muster. That night Eli made me spicy vegetables and told me funny stories about his family, but things felt slightly stilted and uncomfortable, and though he kissed me good-bye when he took me home and said he really liked me and that he'd call the next day, he didn't. He never called again; *I* called after two weeks and bitched him out. Although he had understandable excuses about needing to focus on his career and being afraid of what he was feeling about me (blah blah blah), it didn't change the fact that we weren't going to see each other much anymore. I hung up and took the condom boxes out of the bag and looked at them and laughed, sadly. When would I ever again need extra-large condoms? I couldn't just keep them in the cabinet—I certainly didn't want to make anyone feel inadequate—and I couldn't take them back, although at the time that $20 had been a big splurge and I rather wished I could. I imagined going back to Fantasy Video, saying to the clerk, "You know, I actually didn't use these after all, and it's unlikely I will ever need them."

But the boxes of condoms are still there, and I am actually on friendly terms with Eli, although not friendly enough to tell him what I've hidden in my medicine cabinet, waiting for him to realize he made a mistake. I feel quite lucky to have the recipe for the tossed spicy vegetables, however; each time I make it, it tastes better than the last. Ah, the wisdom that comes with age. Right.

$2^1/_2$ cups broccoli florets
$2^1/_2$ cups cauliflower florets
2 tablespoons olive oil
1 medium onion, sliced
2 tablespoons minced garlic
$^1/_4$ cup chopped fresh parsley
2 tablespoons white wine vinegar
2 heaping teaspoons grated lemon zest
1 teaspoon dried oregano
$^1/_2$ teaspoon dried crushed red pepper
$^1/_2$ cup grated Parmesan cheese
Salt and black pepper

Cook the broccoli and cauliflower in a large saucepan of boiling salted water for about 3 minutes, just until tender. Drain.

Heat the olive oil in a heavy skillet over medium heat. And the onion and garlic and sauté until soft, about 8 minutes. Add the parsley, white wine vinegar, lemon zest, oregano and red pepper, and stir for 2 minutes. Add the vegetables and toss until coated and thoroughly heated. Season the vegetables to taste with salt and pepper. Mix in grated Parmesan and serve immediately.

CONWAY'S CHILES RELLENOS CASSEROLE

Conway was a musician/aspiring ornithologist whose sad, witty songs lodged in my brain and stayed there. Looking back, I see that I was, essentially, a groupie. But while Conway was onstage I loved him with every ounce of my being, and other times, well, I looked forward to when he would be, again, onstage.

He lived in a warehouse with nine other people, and I tolerated all sorts of things I never would now (a disgusting shared bathroom, a continual blanket of cigarette smoke and his roommates' disdain at my poorly disguised admiration) simply to be near such genius. I felt very bohemian waking up in squalor after long nights of drinking and talking about the truly important aspects of life—art, literature and

music. The kitchen (there was one, of sorts) was equally disgusting, but once when I came over I found it spotless, with this casserole in the oven.

Sometimes I still wake up with Conway's songs in my head, and I have fond memories of the tar-papered rooftop where we bird-watched. Although what we had wasn't remotely close to love, I was glad to have briefly visited a world where it didn't matter that the gas bill hadn't been paid for two months or that Gatorade was acceptable sustenance for breakfast, as was the exchange of ideas.

I know that dirt and poverty and cigarettes don't necessarily make art, but they do sometimes contribute to the process.

2 cans (4 ounces each) roasted and peeled green chiles
6 ounces Monterey Jack cheese
6 ounces sharp Cheddar cheese
2 eggs
$1/2$ cup sour cream

Preheat the oven to 350°F. Cover the bottom of an 8- or 9-inch baking dish with a layer of seeded, deveined chiles. Add 1 layer each of the shredded cheeses, then repeat. Beat the eggs slightly and fold in the sour cream. Pour over the casserole and spread evenly. Bake for 30 minutes, or until slightly browned. Yum.

ANDRE'S PARMESAN PESTO DIP

The only thing I remember Andre making me (besides really angry, on a regular basis) is this Parmesan pesto dip, and he made it at least twice a week. He ate it on pita bread, on tortillas, dipped vegetables into it and sometimes simply ate it with a spoon.

I went out with Andre despite his having a tractor named Sue, a ridiculous swagger, and an ex-wife with whom I worked. To be fair, he could also be rather charming and had lovely teeth. Lily, his ex-wife, conceded to these facts, but told me detailed stories about his horrid behavior, and said he'd not once cooked for her the whole time they were married (eleven months). And these things were quite insignificant compared to the other bad things he'd done. But I was achingly, perversely curious about how one man could possibly *be* so awful, so infuriating.

Yet, indeed, he was. Thirty-four years old and living with his fittingly snide and cantankerous mother, Andre was chauvinistic, rude, solipsistic and mean. He was truly awful, the absolute worst. But the laws of physics suggest that his opposite exists, somewhere (not that anyone can find him necessarily, but how heartening to know the perfect man exists—phew, what a relief, and we can finally all stop holding our collective breaths).

BEAUTIFUL

BEAUTIFUL

1/2 cup sour cream
1 cup freshly grated Parmesan cheese
1 tablespoon vegetable oil
1/2 cup mayonnaise
2 tablespoons lemon juice
1 tablespoon finely chopped onion
1/2 cup coarsely chopped watercress
4 tablespoons pesto sauce (bottled is fine)
1 teaspoon Worcestershire sauce
Fresh vegetables for dipping
Salt and pepper

Combine all the ingredients, except for vegetables, and season with salt and pepper to taste. Refrigerate at least 2 hours before serving.

Davis's Spicy Southern BBQ Rub

Traveling across the country together, Davis and I played endless games of Alphabet, sang camp songs and made lists of everything in the world that we loved and hated. We listened to Helen Reddy and had a roaring contest. We bought wigs at a thrift store and wore them in restaurants. Davis had a very loud laugh, and we were kicked out of an International House of Pancakes for "being excessively silly."

Like all people worth loving, Davis had some unfortunate habits, but he was incredibly good to me. In a dirty, cinderblock motel in Indiana he forfeited the baseball game, allowing me to watch a public television special on Gila monsters, *and* went to the nearby convenience store for groceries. He made spicy chicken on a barbecue grill borrowed from the motel's proprietor, a surly, heavyset woman who said she'd rather see all abortion doctors beheaded and strung up on the Empire State Building than legalize the killing of babies. Though unable to alter her thinking, Davis managed, in his patient, gentle way, to soften her a little. He also gave her some of this chicken, which she loved.

He is now working for a nonprofit in New York, and has organized a group that knits scarves and hats for the homeless. I keep a picture of him on my bulletin board above my computer to remind myself not to be so stubborn and blind.

2 tablespoons salt
2 tablespoons granulated sugar
2 tablespoons brown sugar
2 tablespoons cumin
2 tablespoons chili powder
2 tablespoons black pepper
2 tablespoons cayenne (or less if you'd like)
4 tablespoons paprika

Put the spices in a large zippered plastic bag, then throw in 2 pounds of boneless, skinless chicken and "marinate" (shake). Bake the chicken in a 400°F oven for 10 minutes, or grill over a hot fire until done.

WELCOME TO
THE TURTLE BEACH BAR
KO TAO COTTAGE RESORT
5.00 P.M. - 02.00 A.M.
AFTER DO NOTHING FOR
THE WHOLE DAY COME AND
HAVE A REST AFTERWARD

Tom Tung bung
boil a pot of water. add 3
น. H.

AARON'S POST–PEACE CORPS TOM YUM GOONG

After the Peace Corps, I hung out in Thailand with another volunteer in an island bungalow while we tried to figure out what to do with the rest of our lives. We didn't come up with much. We ate soup instead and spent a lot of time angst-ing about the sex we weren't having.

6 cups chicken stock

1 to 2 stalks lemongrass, cut into 2-inch pieces

3 lime leaves (also known as Kaffir lime leaves, or fragrant lime leaves. Look for them in Asian food markets or online at imported foods sites; fresh is best, but they also come dried)

2 shallots or a small red onion, finely chopped

15 to 20 large shrimp, peeled and deveined, but with the tails left on

20 small fresh mushrooms, halved, or 1 can straw mushrooms, drained and trimmed

2 tablespoons fish sauce

1 teaspoon chili sauce

Juice of 1 lime (about 3 tablespoons)

1 bunch cilantro

1 chile pepper, cut into thin rings

Chopped scallions, for garnish

Bring the chicken stock to a boil, then turn down the heat to a simmer. Crush or lightly pound the lemongrass and lime leaves to bring out their flavors and add them to the stock with the shallots. Let it simmer for 5 minutes, then add the shrimp and mushrooms, and simmer another 3 minutes, or just until the shrimp turn pink. Remove from the heat and stir in the fish sauce, chili sauce and lime juice. Garnish with cilantro leaves, chile pepper rings and chopped scallions. Serve hot.

RHETT'S QUESADILLA THINGS

Is it karmic law that at some point everyone has to put in her time with a devastatingly attractive, brilliantly witty, total misogynist jerk who's incredible in bed? He was everything I'd never want in a boyfriend: didactic and argumentative, moody and uncommunicative. He assumed all women read *Cosmo*, was prone to statements such as "You know, I probably know more feminists than you do," and had a habit of trying to arrange me in the poses of recent *Playboy* centerfolds—"just to see how it looks." I conducted myself throughout our brief affair with a combination of detached sarcasm and rabid lust that he seemed to find feisty and fetching.

Rhett didn't cook, per se, but there was one thing he made, and he'd perfected it through daily practice. I make these for myself all the time now, and thankful as I am to be through with the Rhetts of my life (and specifically this one, who I later heard was in prison in California on drug charges—lovely, huh?) my quesadilla things just never quite measure up to my memory of his. Still: you can revamp this recipe depending on what you've got in your fridge; and it's quick, easy and great for just one person.

Refried beans (I use canned ones)
Butter or cooking spray
2 flour tortillas
Grated cheese (Cheddar, Jack, mozz, whatever)
Sliced jalapeños
Salsa
Sour cream

Spread a layer of beans evenly over 1 tortilla, making sure to get as close to the edges as possible. With butter or cooking spray warm a frying pan to medium heat. Make sure the frying pan is big enough to accommodate the aforementioned tortilla. When the pan is hot, plunk the beaned tortilla in it, bean side up. Spread with the cheese, sprinkle on jalapeños and top with the other tortilla. Press down with a spatula the way you would if you were making grilled cheese sandwiches because, basically, you are. Keep checking the down side of the tort. When it's all pretty and golden brown, flip that puppy over and cook her on the other side. (Note: you may have to add some more butter to the pan for the second side. You also may have to keep adjusting the heat so the thing doesn't burn. This is much easier to do on a gas stove than an electric one. If you have an electric stove you probably shouldn't be making this. Electric stoves kind of suck, don't they? I know, I have one.) Anyway, when the second side is golden brown, the cheese should be melted and the beans heated up. To serve you *must* (because this is how Rhett did it) put a big dollop of salsa in the middle with a smaller dab of sour cream on top of it. Then cut into 8 wedges, like a pizza pie.

FRED PINTO'S TACO SOUP

Fred Pinto's mother didn't like me. She didn't like that I was a brunette, that I played soccer (badly), or that my mother wasn't a churchgoer. I was hoping to gain points on prom night, and I actually had her voice in my head when I picked out that horrid sapphire strapless dress and sequined shawl. I was going to charm the pants off her, because I thought I loved her son. We had just eaten dinner at the Beef 'n Brew and stopped back at his house so pictures could be taken, and Fred, having proclaimed that he was in love with me, decided to test that emotion and let me drive his mother's car. I didn't hit anything, but when I stopped I must have forgotten to put on the emergency brake, because as we stood on the porch, gazing at each other, the Blazer rolled out of the driveway. Fred's mother was watching from the window, and ran outside to shriek, "Of all the girls at that lousy school, you spend your hard-earned money on this, this . . . floozy?" She barreled toward me, and I ran around the house and crouched under the back porch. I certainly was not a floozy, or not yet anyway, and I had never before been spoken to in such a manner.

Fred eventually coaxed me out with promises from his father's liquor cabinet, and we skipped the dance and drove out to hills that looked over the lights of the town. We talked about where we most wanted to go in the world, and where we saw ourselves in ten years. We drank a fifth of vodka, smoked a whole pack of Merits and messed around on a blanket on the ground in front of the car. Neither one of us remembered falling asleep, but we were shaken awake by two policemen and Fred's mother not long after sunrise.

Fred wasn't allowed to see me after that, but occasionally we'd get together when his parents or mine were out of town. This was the glorious result of one such encounter.

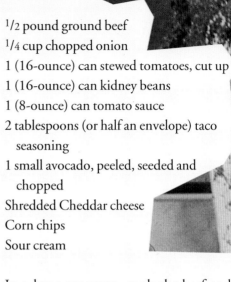

^{1}/2 pound ground beef
^{1}/4 cup chopped onion
1 (16-ounce) can stewed tomatoes, cut up
1 (16-ounce) can kidney beans
1 (8-ounce) can tomato sauce
2 tablespoons (or half an envelope) taco
    seasoning
1 small avocado, peeled, seeded and
    chopped
Shredded Cheddar cheese
Corn chips
Sour cream

In a large saucepan, cook the beef and onion until the meat is brown. Drain excess fat, then add 1^{1}/2 cups water, the tomatoes, beans (don't drain the tomatoes or beans), tomato sauce and taco seasoning. Simmer, covered, for 15 minutes, then add the avocado. Garnish each bowl (makes 6) with cheese, corn chips and sour cream.

BRADY'S PEPPER CHEESE DIP

Brady and I took imaginary trips to exotic locales, and described to each other what we saw and ate and wore. We imagined background music and artistic edits, as if we were constantly watching a movie of our life together that wasn't really our life. In our literal, real-time life, we barely left the two-mile radius around my apartment. We called it the Bermuda Triangle, and it amused us to be so in love that we lost touch with the outside world. Or it amused us to *think* we were so in love with each other that little else mattered. When our relationship was tested—I worked long hours tearing the perforated edges off standardized tests and his ex-girlfriend (with whom he was still incredibly smitten) moved into the Bermuda Triangle—he realized that he had essentially wasted a lot of time taking the said imaginary trips. But no time spent with another person is ever wasted (if I believed that it was I'd have to shoot myself), and in many ways the trip we took to Paris was better than my actual trip to Paris two years later. Walking with Brady along the Seine with imaginary rain falling and ABBA's "Our Last Summer" in my head is still one of my favorite boy memories. Sad, but true.

Brady's mother gave him this pepper cheese dip recipe, which we ate with nearly everything. When you make it you'll immediately understand—I'm serious.

1 (10-ounce) package Monterey Jack cheese
1 (10-ounce) package Monterey Jack cheese with jalapeños
1 can chopped green chiles
1²/₃ cups Hellman's or Best Foods mayonnaise

Preheat the oven to 350°F. Chop or grate the cheeses and stir in the chiles and mayonnaise. Spoon into a casserole and bake for 45 minutes. Serve with tortilla chips or anything else that's languishing in your cupboard.

Perfect Vinaigrette by Arlo

Keith the Pathological Liar's Cold Remedy

Elmer's Spot-Removing Potion

Kurt's BBQ Marinade

Ronald's Ex-Wife's Recipes for Things to Do with
Children on Weekends

The Denorex Guy's Champagne Punch

Slippery Things

Christopher's Cream of Sorrel Soup

Lit. Theory Boy's Caviar Dip

Warren's Butternut Squash Soup

Al's Sizzlin' Nissen

Sandy's Life-Changing Smoothie

Cole the Lepidopterist's Nana's Barley Soup

Today was dull, but relating
I want to know what you are doing
now ... I miss you. So many things
... that remind me of you
... the way people kiss in the movies

POST CARD

ADDRESS

PERFECT VINAIGRETTE BY ARLO

The year I lived with Arlo in a basement apartment in Cleveland, Thanksgiving was spent at a potluck kind of thing for all the orphans, foreigners, stragglers and otherwise disenfranchised people we knew. Being the good girl I am, I called my grandmother in Florida to wish her a happy Thanksgiving and hear all about the gathering at Great-Aunt Minerva and Great-Uncle Elwin's. She asked me what I was doing to celebrate, and I told her about the potluck. "We're bringing the salad," I said.

"I'm also bringing the salad to Minerva's," she cried. "I have it all ready to go. I made a molded salad, I know that's not your kind of salad but that's what I like, a molded salad. And I got a new recipe I tried this time. You take a red Jell-O—I like cherry—and you add a can of crushed pineapple, a can of mandarin orange slices, a jar of the cherries, and also, you use your melon baller to make cream cheese balls and then you roll those in some chopped peanuts and you throw those all in there too and you let that get gelled in your Frigidaire."

"Wow, Grandma," I said, "that's a lot of work you've gone to. Arlo and I just made a green salad. He makes really great dressing."

"Funny you should say that," my grandmother said, "because just as you called I was just getting ready to make the dressing for my salad too. So easy. Half sour cream, half mayonnaise, you blend them and pour it right on over."

Needless to say, that is not the dressing recipe which I now present you.

2 garlic cloves, finely minced
$1/4$ teaspoon salt
$1/4$ teaspoon pepper
1 teaspoon Dijon mustard
1 teaspoon honey
1 tablespoon red wine vinegar
3 tablespoons olive oil

Crush together the garlic, salt and pepper. Add the mustard and honey, and mix well. Add the vinegar and oil, and whisk with a fork until well blended, or do the whole thing in a jar with a lid so you can shake it to mix it very well. It's enough for a salad for two, maybe. Multiply as necessary; all proportions are the same except the salt, which you should just do to taste after $1/2$ teaspoon or so. This dressing keeps well in the fridge, so you can make up a whole bunch and always have it on hand. Arlo would kill me for saying that; he'd insist on making it fresh every time. But he was a little obsessive, and this is my cookbook, not his, goddammit.

KEITH THE PATHOLOGICAL LIAR'S COLD REMEDY

Keith was a heavy-lidded, shaggy-haired poet who sometimes wore his pants inside out, as if to suggest he had much more important things to think about than putting his pants on right. He was one of those boys you resist and then find yourself strangely, strongly, stupidly drawn to. I fell in love with him in a writing workshop when he said he wished my mean mother character was his own mother. And although not one, but two, people warned me that he was a pathological liar, I took no heed. *Ridiculous*, I thought, *I'm a good judge of character*. But then, I'd never known a pathological liar.

Keith told wonderful stories. He'd even won several storytelling contests. Or he said he did. I now believe that nearly everything he ever said to me was a lie in some sense of the word, but this fact doesn't change my appreciation of the stories. My favorite is about the cranky Czech bus driver who'd shoved him out of the bus on a rainy night in Prague. He'd fallen face first onto the street and broken both his front teeth.

"That must have been awful," I said.

"You don't even know the half of it," he said, and sighed heavily, indicating he lived in a world of suffering of which I had no comprehension. (I later found out he'd never been to Prague.)

Keith's best stories were about Samson, the ghost who lived in the attic above his bathroom, and the things they talked about. He also told compelling tales about a man in a pointed yellow hat who followed him around campus, laughing behind his hand, nearly every day.

When I broke up with Keith, he said I was a fickle creature, incapable of honesty or emotion. He then sent me a seven-page, tearstained, slightly hysterical letter written on music paper. I dig it out from time to time to remind myself how lucky I am to be very far away from that beautiful, crazy boy who rarely got sick.

If *you* get sick, try his cold remedy. It really works.

2 shots brandy
8 ounces hot water (nearly boiling)
Juice of 1 lemon
2 tablespoons honey

Repeat as often as necessary.

ELMER'S SPOT-REMOVING POTION

It's beyond me why Elmer even considered for a moment that I was necessary to his existence. He was a marine biologist, fifteen years older than I, and had lived alone (happily) for a long time. Apparently he had spent much of that time perfecting his living space, and I was reprimanded for sitting on an antique chair, glared at for not leaving my shoes on the doorstep, and sighed at for confusing port and Madeira.

Our first camping trip together took place on a very cold, rainy November weekend. Now, when *I* go camping I throw everything into a large backpack and hope all necessary items have been magically included, but Elmer made list after list, and double- and triple-checked them. When packing clothes he folded them, put them in a Ziploc bag and then sucked the air out of the bag like a package of freeze-dried space food. I watched, incredulous. To meet someone who sees the world essentially as a big mess to be cleaned up is pretty interesting when you see it as perfection—that is, until you get there. Then again, that weekend he was warm and dry and I was rather miserable. And he didn't refrain from saying, repeatedly, "I told you so."

Elmer was a great cook, of course—what didn't he do well?—but the most valuable recipe I got from him was this stain-removing potion. I don't know why he even had it, as he was so careful he didn't spill anything, ever. Me, well, that's another story.

1. Soak up a stain with a cloth.
2. Dampen area with cold water, blot, repeat several times.
3. Mix $1/2$ teaspoon detergent powder in 1 cup lukewarm water. Pour some on the area, scrub lightly; blot with a paper towel. Repeat until the cup is empty.
4. Blend $1/4$ cup white vinegar with $1/2$ cup water. Pour over the area, then, 2 to 4 minutes later, blot.

Kurt's BBQ Marinade

Kurt was a bastard, and it makes me so mad even to think about him that I can't begin to tell about what a lowlife he is. Suffice it to say that our story involves lots of alcohol, far too much money spent on various means of travel, and the very tardy realization that I, in Kurt's mind, was not one of a kind, but one of a whole brood of women he kept ties to in case one of us might come in handy. He is a despicable human being and I hope I never lay eyes on him again as long as I live. (So, okay, fine, he made good marinade. It was the only decent thing he ever did in his pitiful, pathetic, repugnant life!)

All ingredients are approximate and the recipe should be multiplied to great quantities because barbecues are more fun when there are lots of people and lots of food.

> $^1/_4$ cup dark soy sauce
> $^1/_4$ cup honey
> $^1/_8$ cup sherry
> 3 tablespoons minced garlic

Kurt, slime-lord though he may be, used to marinate thick slices of eggplant and rings of sweet onion, chunks of zucchini and squash, and sometimes fresh tuna (it's orgiastic!). But you can toss in whatever you like. The longer it marinates, the better it tastes. I can't tell you much about how to cook it, because I always let Kurt do the barbecuing part, since it seemed to threaten his masculinity if I even got near a bag of charcoal, let alone something so virile and manly as lighter fluid. Now I think I stay away from barbecues altogether just because they make me think of him, which tends to take away my appetite.

I actually liked him at first, too. That's the part that kills me. Seduced by marinated tuna! It's pathetic. (But delicious . . .)

RONALD'S EX-WIFE'S RECIPES FOR THINGS TO DO WITH CHILDREN ON WEEKENDS

Ronald had custody of his two small children on weekends, which, as I worked nights, were the only times I could see him. He was a dedicated, wonderful father, which can make one ignore all sorts of very obvious incompatibilities. And I was crazy about his kids, Sarah and Tyler.

Ronald felt that education at public school was barely adequate, but as he didn't have the means to send the kids to private school, took it upon himself to fill in the enormous gaps in their learning. He paced around the kitchen, lecturing, while Sarah, Tyler and I made a terrific mess with Play-Doh, finger paints and papier-mâché. I don't think they were old enough then to absorb the staggering amount of American history Ronald covered, though he filled a lot of *my* educational gaps.

Papier-Mâché
Shredded newspaper
Salt
Flour
Plastic container

Soak the shredded newspaper in cold water in a plastic container. Stir the mixture with a wooden spoon. Make a heavy paste with the flour, cold water and a small quantity of salt. Mix this paste with the paper pulp. Stir until pliable. Spread over the base of balloons, wire, wood or anything else you want.

Finger Paint

$1^1/2$ cups laundry starch
1 quart boiling water
$1^1/2$ cups soap flakes
Screw-top jars
$1/2$ cup talc (optional)
$1/2$ tablespoon poster paint or dry pigment of whatever colors you want

Mix the starch with cold water to form a creamy paste. Add the boiling water and cook until transparent or glossy. Stir constantly. Add the talc, if you want to make the mixture smoother. Let the mixture cool, and add the soap flakes and stir. Let cool and put in the jars; stir poster paint in each jar.

Play-Doh

Water
1 cup salt
2 cups flour
2 tablespoons olive oil
Food coloring
Plastic bags

Add water slowly to the salt, flour and olive oil. Knead the mixture until doughy. Divide into portions and add color with a few drops of food coloring. Stir and refrigerate.

THE DENOREX GUY'S
CHAMPAGNE PUNCH

One year for Halloween Erin dressed up as the artist Frida Kahlo. It was a fabulous costume: turban, eyebrows, mustache, hoop earrings and all. The only other truly inventive costume that year—aside from our friends Caren and Ally, who went as Nancy Kerrigan and Tonya Harding, both wearing Ally's old ice skating costumes from when she took lessons in eighth grade, Caren's knee bandaged, Ally wielding a lead pipe like some lost murderess from the game of Clue—was the guy hosting the party, who wore a bathrobe and parted his hair very deliberately down the middle, one half his head sudsed up in white foam, the other half minty green. I was dressed as Miss Ace Hardware 1947, which just meant I looked slutty in a

vaguely historical pinup calendar sort of way. I got completely tanked on the Denorex Guy's champagne punch, proceeded to forget that it was Halloween at all, and lunged at the poor man at midnight demanding a New Year's kiss.
He responded politely, if not with quite the passion I'd hoped for, and returned me to Erin's care for the remainder of the evening. It was Caren who actually woke up in the Denorex Guy's bed the next morning, wearing nothing, she told us later, except her silver medal.

Okay, fine, I know one pretty-much-unreciprocated kiss does not an ex-boyfriend make. Can you please just go with it, though, for the sake of the punch?

$1/2$ cup sugar, dissolved in hot water
One 6-ounce can orange juice concentrate
1 pint orange sherbet
1 quart cranberry juice cocktail
1 quart ginger ale
1 bottle champagne
1 cup fresh lemon juice (squeeze it yourself, or you'll be really sorry)
A few cups of ice

Mix together all ingredients in a big punch bowl. Serve.

129

CHRISTOPHER'S CREAM
OF SORREL SOUP

After dating Milo (see Milo Burda's Amazing Bean Soup in Substantial Things), who had absolutely no interest in current pop-cultural phenomena and refused to listen to any music recorded after 1980 or watch current-run movies, I met a very cultured and erudite older man named Christopher at a coffee shop. (If you must know, I spilled my coffee on his newspaper.) We went to openings and lectures and museums and hip costume parties and cool jazz clubs, and although I enjoyed it all very much, I began to be irritated by the fact that he so obviously felt he had to be up on *everything*. Perhaps his behavior irritated me simply because it brought my own laziness and complacency into *bas-relief*, but no one can possibly *ever* keep up with everything, just as at some point one must realize that she will never be able to read all the books she wants to in the span of her life. There are plenty of things to be guilty about—not keeping up with what's hip should not be one of them. Plus, I was exhausted.

Christopher and I mostly dined out, either at up-and-coming or old and well-regarded restaurants, but he once made this lovely soup, which we enjoyed *sans* fanfare (for once).

^{1}/3 cup minced yellow onions

3 tablespoons butter

^{3}/4 cup fresh sorrel

^{1}/2 teaspoon salt

3 tablespoons flour

5^1/2 cups chicken broth, boiling

2 egg yolks

^{1}/2 cup whipping cream

^{1}/2 tablespoon butter

Cook the onions in the butter in a covered saucepan for 5 to 10 minutes until the onions are translucent but not browned. Stir in the sorrel and salt, cover, and cook for 5 minutes on low heat. Sprinkle in the flour and stir over moderate heat for 3 minutes. Stir in the hot chicken broth, then turn off the heat.

Put the mixture into a blender or food processor and puree, then return it to the saucepan. In a large mixing bowl, blend the egg yolks and whipping cream. Take a cup of soup and whisk it into the bowl, then slowly dribble the mixture into the pan. Stir in the softened butter. Decorate with a nasturtium blossom, and serve with a flourish.

LIT. THEORY BOY'S CAVIAR DIP

In college, during a lit. theory class that inspired analogies to incarceration, *Middlemarch* and other various forms of torture, I sat next to an adorable boy who was absolutely the only reason I didn't change my major right then and there. At first, we passed notes to pass the time through excruciating and interminable lectures, then started having dinner together after class to blow off pent-up rage and frustration. Finally, we moved on to meeting before class to prepare each other for the ensuing onslaught of Foucault and Lacan. One afternoon in April, as the campus bell tower tolled, announcing the impending insufferableness, we found ourselves somewhat acrobatically entwined in the sheets of his twin bed, seemingly prepared to do *anything* so as to render ourselves incapable of attending that class. It became clear to us that we'd made a profound discovery: *sex is actually the antidote to literary theory.*

This caviar dip is something he made for me during one of our early adventures in truancy, and I was awed by it. The recipe, it turned out, he'd gotten off the Internet. Go figure. Regardless, it's delicious. I like to serve it with Carr's Table Water Crackers or, if you like something a little more flaky and flavorful, Breton Crackers. Lit. Theory Boy served it with baby carrots and Ritz crackers, but only because that's all he could find in our little college town. Maybe he ordered the caviar off the Internet too?

1 cup sour cream

2 scallions, sliced very thinly

1 tablespoon fresh lemon juice (please don't use ReaLemon; it's not convenient, it's just gross)

1 tablespoon (plus a little extra for garnish) fresh chives (although he never put chives in his; might as well have called for fairy dust for all that fresh herbs were available to us then)

1/4 cup caviar, drained (and save a bit for garnish)

Mix the sour cream, scallions, lemon juice and chives. Add the caviar gently. Sprinkle with extra chives and caviar, so it looks pretty, you know.

WARREN'S BUTTERNUT
SQUASH SOUP

Warren lived in my dorm and although I'd noticed him, barefoot, in the dining hall, our first real encounter was in the library. We were sitting on either side of a tall desk partition, and about twenty minutes after he'd sat down, Warren handed me this note, written on technical paper:

Though I am sure I have broken your concentration and made it difficult to study, I must tell you this is not what I had intended. You see, I have been distracted, so distracted that I am unable to study myself. I hoped that this approach would, at least in part, be an answer to both problems. I do not blame the circumstances, only myself, and despite the complete awkwardness of this situation, would like to talk to you in the near future. I do but hardly know you, but it has been enough for me to conclude that you are not the average sorority girl. In fact, I do not believe you are a sorority girl at all. Perhaps you are, and if that is the case, do not be offended—for who am I to judge after only eating lunch near you once? It is also likely that my perception of sororities is skued [sic]. Whether you are or are not does not matter I guess. No, it really doesn't.

Instead of wishing I had not risked this encounter and ended up on the other side of a table partition, I have decided to attempt to ease your alarm with this note and with that renew your concentration and my own.

I believe it has been established that we both have bicycles, and I would like it very much if you would ride and talk with me. I do not know what time you usually get up, but I will be leaving for work around 9 A.M. If you accept this invitation please come to room 601 around 7:30 and we will go. If you do not accept I will go by myself, and though disappointed, I will not suffer from breathing the early-morning air. I apologize both for the technical nature of this sheet of paper and for the alarm my presence may have given you. Realize that I am asking nothing more than a chance to know more about you than what I have been told.

The first and only time we went camping together, Warren sprinted around like a dog who'd been in a too-small kennel for days. He climbed trees and fanned the campfire with enormous, foul-smelling leaves. He lassoed stumps, the sticking-out bumper of my van, his dog, Sally, and me. After I yelled at him and he calmed down a little, he reheated this wonderful soup on his Coleman stove.

2 medium butternut squash
Butter
Thyme
1 yellow onion, diced
Salt and white pepper
Chives
Crème fraîche

Peel, seed and dice the squash. In a small saucepan, slice a small dollop of butter into an inch of water. Add a pinch (or more) of thyme, then put in the squash and the yellow onion, and cook, covered, until soft. Pour the mixture into a blender or press through a strainer, add salt and pepper. Top with chives and crème fraîche, if you want to get fancy.

HOW TO GET TO THE FARMHOUSE – a novel

Prologue: watch out for cats as you approach the house.

...pter the First: in which our heroine, having chosen Highway 2, takes t... ...est route. Take highway 2 east. About 8 miles out of town it makes a ...e to the right (curve signs, 40 mph signs etc) but you're going to KE... NG STRAIGHT (after checking carefully for oncoming cars in the oppo... ...which you'll be crossing – your safety is important to us). N... ...road OASIS (name precedes band): it curves left. Take ... ...0ᵗʰ St., a gra... ...ter the Sec... Make a right and go another 3/... ...catine out of ... ...roximately 2.735 miles after s... ...here used to be a sign, but it w... ...l sure to wreck the bottom of your car. There used to be a sign, but it w... ...en by looters in the wake of the Rodney King riots (and you thought Iowa... ...re apathetic!) Note the innocuous beige house on the corner. Go 1.8 mil... ...ere's a big pasture of black cows on your right and you'll see the Junk Hous... ...the corner of 940ᵗʰ and Oasis (and you'll see why it's called the Junk Hous... ...ake a right on Oasis and go one miles, in the course of which you will cro... ...ilroad tracks, be tempted by the devil and discover the heal... ...ffects of herb... Chapter the Third: in which our heroine, for some utterly inexplicable... ...wants to take the Interstate. Save yourself the trouble and opt for 1 or 2...

AL'S SIZZLIN' NISSEN

I once dated a guy named Al who organized a huge barbecue party for my twenty-seventh birthday at the farmhouse where Erin and I lived. The directions he handed out on how to get there were probably worth the trip alone, and Al's illustrations (somewhat pre-schoolian in nature) were one of a kind. Al promised that revelers would be treated to his own special drink, dubbed "The Sizzlin' Nissen." And here's how she sizzled . . .

"At length burst in the argen... With plume, tiara and all ri... --John Keats

...vance Critical Acclaim for Thisbe's Birthday Barbecue

"We live here, but even if we didn't we'd come to the barbecue." -- Georgianna, Erin and Tom, *The Farmhouse Gazette*

"Judging from her other birthdays, this promis...

1 cup frozen strawberries
$1/2$ cup frozen raspberries
1 kiwi
1 cup vodka
7Up, or like-minded fizzy water

Blend all ingredients except the fizzy water in a blender. Add the fizzy water, to taste. Al says that if you're really feeling like tying one on, add rum too. But don't blame me, or him, if your head hurts like hell tomorrow morning.

That This be'sa live one!

evelry, array"

What kind of food is everybody bringing?"
-- Connie Brothers, The Iowa Writers' Workshop

Sizzlin' Nis

to be one more."

poison pen!"

SANDY'S LIFE-CHANGING SMOOTHIE

Like so many romantic and hopeful people, I am a sucker. Anyone who knows me knows how easily enamored I am of the next best thing, whether it be the Eat 4 Your Blood Type diet (a sham!), the Tae-Bo workout (when the tapes still cost $100 a set—cripes!) or a new and "but-he's-different-than-the-others" boyfriend.

Sandy was a sensitive, alcoholic EMT who matched my enthusiasm toward anything promising physical or emotional health, strength, happiness or clarity. He had been drinking the same smoothie every morning for twelve years (okay, once he was in India and went without a smoothie for three weeks) and claimed it was the reason that he never got sick, could drink a twelve-pack with no adverse effect, had lovely skin and was so good in bed. He didn't actually claim that last part, but I know he believed it. He also believed he had to speak to his mother on the phone every day and that his tight, acid-washed jeans looked sexy.

I had to let him go, but I still make one of these every morning. No promises, but it's a good way to start the day.

1 banana
1 cup 2% milk
$^{1}/_{2}$ cup orange juice
Handful of frozen strawberries
1 teaspoon vanilla extract
$^{1}/_{2}$ teaspoon cinnamon
Ice cubes
(Sandy added a raw egg, but it's not necessary)

Blend! Drink! Be well!

COLE THE LEPIDOPTERIST'S NANA'S BARLEY SOUP

Cole was a butterfly collector who lived in a tiny apartment right by the Broadway–Lafayette Street subway station. What his apartment lacked in size, it made up for in huge beautiful old windows that seemed to change the light as it filtered in. Even on overcast or glaring days, the sun seemed to come into his room calmly glowing. Cole loved the light—I'm sure it was the only reason he stayed in that cramped studio—and didn't like to cover the windows, but he was paranoid that people were looking in, watching him. Cole was an angelic boy, fair and fragile, and New York didn't do wonders for his nerves. He always talked about getting out, and I hope he did one day. He should have been somewhere with fewer people and more butterflies.

4 to 6 rosy soup bones (just ask your butcher)
$1/2$ cup pea or navy beans
$1/4$ cup barley
$1/2$ cup split peas
1 large onion, chopped
1 tablespoon salt
$1^{1}/2$ cups diced celery
1 carrot, grated

Put the bones in 2 quarts of water and bring to a boil. Skim the gunk off the top as it collects. Add the pea beans and barley. Simmer for 1 hour. Add the split peas, onion and salt, and simmer another hour and 10 minutes. Add the celery and simmer another 20 minutes. Add the carrot and simmer another 3 minutes. Remove the bones and serve.

Trenton Haverford's Lasagna

Seth's Ratatouille

Bailey's Flank Steak

Gary's Brown Derby Cobb Salad

Tommy Nordeng's Mac and Cheese

Phil's Perfect Picadillo

Leroy's Italian Soup

Sven Baylor's Too-Good-to-Be-True Beef Stroganoff

Substantial Things

Ezra's Sticky Chicken

Ziegfried's Authentic Spanish Tortilla

Smitty's Smoked Turkey

Milo Burda's Amazing Bean Soup

Lewis's 20-Cloves-of-Garlic Chicken

Vito's Veggie Galette

Softball Calvin's Tuna Casserole

Fernanda's Boyfriend Bert's Hunky Bran Muffins

TRENTON HAVERFORD'S LASAGNA

Trenton, the first of the two people who have broken my heart, told me he'd started dating me simply out of curiosity. He was a writer and had learned, from a friend of his I'd dated, that behind me was a trail of broken hearts. "I wanted to see how you did it," he said. "You know, how it happened? A study, if you will."

Cold, cold, cold, though I'm sure I've been colder since. And because I am, like so many of us, a glutton for punishment, that conversation was not the end of our relationship. I ignored all the things my friends, parents and therapist said, and continued to love Trenton. No one else has ever made me act like a blindfolded stalker, certain I'd eventually see the things I was looking for in him. He was the kind of guy that makes you smack your forehead, hard, hissing at yourself, "Stupid, stupid, *stupid*."

Trenton had a jagged hole in the ceiling of his bedroom where the rain had ruined the plaster, a shower curtain smeared with black mold, and heaps of clothes masking the furniture of his apartment. But his kitchen was spotless. He didn't like anyone else to set foot in his kitchen, let alone use his knives or pans. But once, at three in the morning, pressed for time, he let me help make lasagna for his dinner party (to which I was only incidentally invited). He called me his ricotta girl, kissed my bare toes and said I had the most beautiful eyebrows he'd ever seen. I think that one night of kindness and passion has been more damaging than any of the horrible stuff I could tell people to make them laugh incredulously.

But the lasagna was perfect. It really was.

3 tablespoons olive oil
1/2 cup chopped onion
1/3 cup chopped carrot

3 garlic cloves, minced
1 pound lean ground beef
3 cups canned Italian plum tomatoes
3 tablespoons butter, melted
1 teaspoon dried oregano, crumbled
1 tablespoon dried basil, crumbled
1 teaspoon salt
$1/2$ teaspoon freshly ground black pepper
$1/2$ pound lasagna noodles, cooked
$1/2$ pound mozzarella cheese, grated
2 cups ricotta cheese
$1/4$ pound freshly grated Parmesan cheese

Preheat the oven to 375°F. Heat the oil in a heavy skillet. Add the onion, carrot and garlic, and cook, stirring, until lightly browned. Push to the side of the pan and add the beef. Break it up into bits, cooking until it loses its pink color. Puree the tomatoes in a blender, add the meat, and simmer 15 minutes. Add the butter, oregano, basil, salt and pepper; partially cover and simmer 30 minutes.

Assemble the lasagna by drizzling some sauce over the bottom of a shallow rectangular baking dish. Put in a layer of noodles, sprinkle with some of the mozzarella, and spread on a layer of ricotta. Make another layer of noodles, sauce, mozzarella and ricotta. Finish with noodles and sauce. Throw caution to the wind and let Trenton kiss your feet. Sprinkle Parmesan evenly over the top and bake 20 minutes, or until hot and bubbling.

SETH'S RATATOUILLE

The first mistake I made with Seth was buying a movie and video guide that contained "more than 2,000 entries, including 300 new entries" and making a (very long) list of movies to view together. We were already well into the movie-watching stage because he worked too much and was always tired, but somehow mentioning that I had made this list implied that I was taking our relationship too seriously. I probably was. But he was the first guy with good grammar I'd met in months. I made the list because I figured we might as well watch worthwhile movies if we were going to spend so much money at the video store and also because I was putting off writing my 101 syllabus.

Seth was no great chef but suddenly, afraid to rent movies with me, he began cooking elaborate meals that required a lot of chopping. When the downhill slide of a romance becomes perceptible, one reads all sorts of things into another's actions. I thought: *He wants to keep his hands busy, away from me.* And because he'd spent so much time on the meal, I always offered to clean up, which kept my hands busy and away from him. Thus the passive-aggressive dance of nonverbal communication continued until we were barely speaking, much less actually enjoying each other.

But one night, our last, over too many bottles of wine and this incredible ratatouille, we finally talked, *really* talked, about everything. Neither one of us had been on the same page, or even reading the same book. He thought I was screwing around, and I thought he was wishing I was. It was too late, finally, but whenever I make this I think of that boozy, painful and poignant night, with the candlelight flickering over his sweet face. So make this for someone you love, and for mercy's sake, communicate!

3 tablespoons olive oil
2 cups thinly sliced sweet onion
2 garlic cloves, minced
Salt and pepper
4 cups peeled eggplant, cut into $3/4$-inch cubes
2 cups coarsely chopped green bell pepper
2 cups small zucchini, sliced $1/2$ inch thick
One 14.5-ounce can diced tomatoes, undrained

Heat the oil in a 4-quart heavy saucepan. Sauté the onion and garlic, then stir in the remaining ingredients. Bring to a boil, then reduce the heat and simmer, covered, for 8 to 10 minutes, or until all the vegetables are tender. Uncover and simmer for 2 to 3 minutes longer until thickened slightly. Season to taste. Serves 8.

BAILEY'S FLANK STEAK

The first time I saw Bailey he was standing in front of the butcher's case at Fred Meyer's, agonizing over which cut of meat to buy for his mother, who was visiting from California. That was endearing, as was almost every other thing about him until I realized that not only was his romantic history as lengthy and ridiculous as mine, but that one of his exes had tried to commit suicide and two others had restraining orders against him. "That was a long time ago," he said, a little too patiently.

The next time his mother came to visit, however, he cooked for both of us, and she got very drunk on red wine and started taunting him, shrieking, "You're an animal! You're a fiend!" and then locked herself in the bathroom for nearly an hour.

I fled. Perhaps there was some Oedipal stuff going on, but inherently I trust mothers more than boyfriends, and I escaped with only a psychic scar or two and this recipe.

Trim steak of fat, and make crisscross lines on each side with a sharp knife. Make the cuts $1/8$ piece inch deep. Combine 2 tablespoons each soy sauce and lemon juice; pour over the meat and marinate for an hour. Barbecue or broil, then slice on the diagonal.

Gary's Brown Derby Cobb Salad

Gary had a little problem with cocaine that I wasn't really aware of until he called me from prison and told me the whole story (*thanks*, Gary). He didn't know how long he'd be incarcerated, and, suspicious that the Feds would destroy his stuff while he was gone, he sent me a box of his mother's recipes. She'd divorced his father and moved to Florida, vowing never to cook again, and I spent many days examining those recipes, the writing, fine chicken scratches and tiny, neat loops that I could make no sense of without my reading glasses. An entire life lived in this recipe box, or rather, a life of disappointments, of which Gary was only one.

Dressing
1 cup water
1 cup red wine vinegar
1 tablespoon sugar
$^1/_2$ tablespoon lemon juice

1 1/2 teaspoons salt

1 tablespoon pepper

1 tablespoon Worcestershire sauce

1 tablespoon English mustard

2 garlic cloves

2 cups olive oil

1 cup salad oil

Blend all the ingredients in a food processor.

For the salad

6 strips cooked bacon

2 peeled, diced tomatoes

2 cooked chicken breasts, diced

6 cups shredded lettuce

1 avocado, diced

3 eggs, hard-boiled and diced

2 tablespoons chives, chopped

1/2 cup bleu cheese, crumbled

Toss with dressing. Right, as if you didn't realize what the next step was.

TOMMY NORDENG'S
MAC AND CHEESE

Tommy was my summer camp boyfriend between fifth and sixth grades. I'd been warned away from him by the other girls, who said he was a no-good ladies' man and that the summer before he'd tried to go up Alice Messinger's shirt. I didn't buy it, not least because Alice was still completely flat-chested, and the story sounded like it was all blown out of proportion. So when Tommy asked if I wanted to take a walk behind the barn during a camp social, I shrugged, *sure*, set down my bug juice and followed him outside. The black flies were particularly bad that summer, swarming around our heads and chomping at the flesh just below the hairline. We waded through the overgrown dandelions and around the back of the barn. And then I'm not sure exactly how what happened happened, but I must have swallowed a black fly because when Tommy turned around suddenly, faced me and stuck his tongue into my mouth, I gagged and started coughing uncontrollably. Tommy sort of pushed me away and stepped back, and I remember him standing there staring at me like I had just thrown up on him or revealed that I had three tongues. Before my coughing subsided, Tommy turned and walked away, and for the next six summers, we never again acknowledged one another's presence.

This wasn't actually his recipe, but it was his absolute favorite camp meal. He once ate six servings. That was back when I still liked him, and I was very impressed.

2 cups elbow macaroni
2 slices whole wheat bread
3 tablespoons butter
3 tablespoons flour
1 cup milk
1 cup vegetable broth
2 cups shredded Cheddar cheese

Cook the macaroni, but don't let it get too soft (al dente, as they say). Finely grind the bread in a food processor.

Melt the butter in a saucepan. Stir 1 tablespoon of the butter into the crumbs.

Add the flour to the remaining 2 tablespoons butter. Heat over a medium flame for 2 minutes, whisking all the while. Gradually add the milk and broth, and whisk another 2 minutes before removing from the flame. Add the cheese and stir until melted. Mix the mac into the sauce and transfer to a baking pan. Top with salt and pepper to taste, and sprinkle on the bread-crumb mixture. Stick under the broiler for 2 minutes, or until crumbs are browned.

PHIL'S PERFECT PICADILLO

Phil was my fellow student in Writing 121, and though the seat chosen on the first day tended to be where nearly everyone stayed all semester, Phil sat in a different seat every day. At first, I thought he was simply daring and original (and handsome), but eventually realized he was slowly circling me, getting closer and closer every day, until he was sitting directly behind me. That day I could feel his breath on my hair, and my arms and fingers went tingly. There were three minutes left in class when I felt a point of cold on the back of my neck and I turned around; Phil was holding a ballpoint pen and blushing. "I'm writing you a note," he whispered. "Turn back around."

I did, and he pulled aside my hair to write. After class I asked Natasha, the department secretary, to tell me what it said. Phil had written FOOD? 753-0371. He said later he'd wanted to write hors d'oeuvre, but couldn't remember the spelling. "If I'd misspelled it, you probably would have thought I was a weirdo. Am I wrong?"

And he never was, really. Eight months later, at the airport, when he was leaving for Spain to study flamenco guitar and I was weeping inconsolably, he put his hand to my cheek and asked, "Sweetie, do you really see us together forever?"

I didn't; of course I didn't, but he was my first love and I hadn't yet learned to think about relationships pragmatically. I've received only three Semana Santa postcards from him in the last eight years, but I trust he is wise, happy and still making this picadillo for his Spanish wife and mistress.

Erin,
Thank you for being patient with me.
I like being with you.
Phil

154

$^1/_2$ cup olive oil

2 pounds ground round

2 medium onions, diced

2$^3/_4$ cups pizza sauce

1 large red bell pepper, diced

$^3/_4$ cup whole tomatoes, drained, cut small

3 garlic cloves, diced

$^1/_3$ cup white vinegar

$^1/_3$ cup manzanilla olives

$^1/_2$ teaspoon oregano

1 cup seedless raisins

1 small bottle capers

Cayenne and salt to taste

Heat the oil in a heavy skillet. Crumble the ground beef coarsely and add to the hot oil. Stir until the meat has changed color, but do not brown. Add the onions to the meat, and allow to simmer for a few minutes. Transfer to a casserole dish or big pan. Add the remaining ingredients except the olives, raisins and capers. Let simmer on low heat for an hour. Remove any excess fat that may accumulate. Add the olives, raisins and capers 20 minutes before cooking is finished, and season to taste.

LEROY'S ITALIAN SOUP

Because I have a terrible memory, I often make copies of important letters before I send them. I rarely reread them, but as this book required it, I went through two boxes of correspondence to and from, and I was reminded, nakedly, how giddy I have been about the possibility of love, willing to try and try, again and again. This is certainly why we celebrate these boys, these past relationships. They were everything, at one time. Their smell and intonation and desire were swimming in us, and it is only proper, as Joan Didion wisely said, to stay on nodding terms with a former self, and revere a former friend or lover.

Leroy is one of the boys I find myself thinking about from time to time, and wondering *how did such deep feelings exist and how have I forgotten them?* I still have the bundle of letters he wrote me from Alaska, when he spent a summer working at a cannery. Perhaps the horrid circumstances in which he worked fueled his ardor for me, but his absence definitely fueled mine for him.

The night he returned we made this Italian soup, and though neither one of us could entirely focus on our food, it was the best meal I'd had in months. We spent a blissed-out week, and then Leroy took the money he'd made (blood money, as he called it), bought a Harley and headed out west to find himself, promising to write as often as he had from Alaska.

Weeks passed, then months. Many, many months. Apparently Leroy didn't miss me as much as he had during those fish guts–filled days. When I saw him by chance four years later at a Motel 6 in Grand Island, Nebraska, I was quite glad he'd neglected our correspondence.

2 ounces bacon
$1/4$ pound ground beef
2 celery stalks
$1/2$ small head cabbage
1 small onion
2 carrots
2 tomatoes

2 bouillon cubes
1 cup peas (fresh or frozen)
1 can kidney beans, rinsed
$1/2$ cup uncooked rice
1 garlic clove, minced
Salt and pepper

Chop the bacon and cook in a skillet. Add the beef and brown. Chop the celery, cabbage, onion, carrots and tomatoes. Add a little water to the bouillon cubes, and then add the peas, beans, rice, garlic and 1 quart water. Cover and cook 45 minutes. Season to taste.

SVEN BAYLOR'S TOO-GOOD-TO-BE-TRUE BEEF STROGANOFF

Until I die I will think fondly of the evening Sven Baylor picked me up after my shift at Orange Julius and we drove north through Redmond, and then west into the reddish glow toward Odin Falls. I was sixteen, and I don't remember what we did that night, or what we talked about, but I remember the drive—Sven's window was stuck down, and the warm air rushed in, lifting away the song on the radio. When I think of freedom, it is of my arm touching his, the smell of our summery skin, the glare of the sun through the windshield, night falling.

Nine years later, I unexpectedly ran into Sven at a friend's pink elephant party, and we got reacquainted while fighting over a blue glass ashtray from Bubba's Brake & Clutch. Sven invited me over for dinner the next night and, with two bottles of good wine, I arrived to find him already plowed, wearing a T-shirt that said *I'M GOING FUCKING NUTS!* I should have gone home immediately, but my anticipation and expectation had reached such a fevered pitch that I could barely see straight. After nine years probably nothing could have satisfied me but, still, a little romance, a little foreplay and a speck of sobriety might have helped the outcome of that night, which truly does not bear repeating. The only thing that rescued a dismal failure was the beef Stroganoff that he'd miraculously made before I arrived. It's my new fantasy, one that has, so far, never disappointed.

6 tablespoons butter
2 tablespoons minced onion
2 pounds beef tenderloin, cut thin in 1- by 1 1/2-inch strips
1/2 pound mushrooms, sliced

Salt and freshly ground black pepper
$^1/_8$ teaspoon nutmeg
1 cup sour cream, at room temperature

Melt 3 tablespoons of the butter in a heavy skillet. Add the onions and cook slowly until transparent, then remove from the heat and set aside. Turn the heat to medium-high, add the beef and cook briefly, turning to brown on all sides. Remove the beef and set aside with the onions. Add the remaining 3 tablespoons of butter to the skillet. Stir in the mushrooms, cover and cook 3 minutes. Season with salt, pepper and nutmeg. Whisk the sour cream and add it to the pan, but don't allow it to boil. Add the beef and onions to the pan and heat. Wonderful.

Sticky Chicken

½ cup vinegar
½ cup sugar
½ cup soy sauce
4½ lbs chicken pieces
2 garlic cloves minced
1 tbs mined fresh ginger

Combine vinegar, sugar and soy. marinate chicken
fridge.

Transfer to skillet. Add garlicn and ginger. Bri
medium heat. Simmer 15 minuites or until chicken
Transfer chikcen to dish an dput in oven to keep w

160

Increase heat ao medium and cook marinade to carm
that it doesn burn-- about 25 minutes.   Return cl
and coat with sauce

EZRA'S STICKY CHICKEN

Like Sean (see The Orchard Boy's Berry Cobbler in Sweet Things), I met Ezra at a farmers' market where I sold fruits and vegetables and herbs and he sold organic free-range chickens. Our booths were directly across from each other, and before we'd ever spoken we passed the slow market hours by making eyes at each other over the bunched spinach and baskets of pattypan squash. When the customer rush began we sent each other knowing glances over the bustle whenever we had a second. And after the closing whistle sounded, he tromped across the way and asked me if I'd like to come for dinner on his farm before I went home to mine. I accepted. After dinner—this delicious sticky chicken—Ezra and I walked across the fields to the pond, stripped down and swam out to the old moored wooden dock. I'm not even going to go into the whole issue of the splinters, just know that they were painful, and that you should think twice before engaging in frictional activity on decaying wooden structures. When we got back to the farmhouse, Ezra took great pains to type out the sticky chicken recipe for me on an old manual typewriter.

veright. in

to boil. over
uns clear.
m. low oven.

ize. Watch
kcn to skillet

ZIEGFRIED'S AUTHENTIC SPANISH TORTILLA

Ziegfried was like a plague on my house. My roommates hated him; no matter how hard he tried to be conversational and friendly, he succeeded only in being rude and condescending. At a Sunday morning house-meeting, my roommates tried to ban him from the premises. "He's a smug bastard," Jessy said. "Exactly!" Amanda said. I defended him, claiming he was shy, but he truly just did not know how to relate to people. "Well, perhaps he should live where other people *don't*," Jessy said. "Like Mars," Amanda said, triumphantly.

For all his faults, which I don't have the space or energy to list, Ziegfried had the ability to laugh at himself. Actually, that was one of his faults as well—he laughed when what he'd said or done or thought wasn't really funny at all. But he had traveled extensively, and had lived in southern Spain for two years, so this recipe is the real thing.

4 to 5 large russet potatoes
2 tablespoons olive oil
1 onion, diced
Salt, to taste
4 large eggs

Peel and cube the potatoes, then fry in the olive oil for about 15 minutes, adding the onion about 10 minutes into the frying. Cook until brown, stirring occasionally, and, once cooked, remove from the heat.

In a separate bowl, beat the eggs and then add the potato mixture. Return to the heated (and cleaned) frying pan with a drop of olive oil. After 5 to 7 minutes, using a flat plate the same circumference as the frying pan, turn the mixture over, allowing it to cook on the other side for another 5 minutes. Remove from the heat and allow to cool for $1/2$ hour. Serve with bread *¡y copita de Jerez, por supuesto!*

SMITTY'S SMOKED TURKEY

Thanksgiving just isn't Thanksgiving without a few key items: Grandma's cranberry relish, canned cranberry sauce (I insist), mini-marshmallow baked yams, extra stuffing, and now: sweet Smitty's Smoked Turkey. He made it once for me; I've made it many times on many different occasions with a host of different boys and friends. But it was Smitty's recipe first. Even though the page on which he wrote out the directions for me is torn and grease-stained, I'll quote his instructions directly here, since no one explains the process better than Smitty. The turkey is cooked in an outdoor grill, which you use as a smoker.

It's hard to screw this recipe up, and you get to hang out inside drinking Bloody Marys. (See Lawry's Bloody Marys in Spicy Things). But please be careful, since drinking Bloody Marys can lead to making out in the bathroom with the guy who mixed them, which can lead to Smitty not wanting to date you anymore, which might make you very sad and regretful. Oh, but that's my story, not yours, right?

"Buy one bag of hickory chips and soak in water at least 24 hours prior to smoking.

"Turkey: Make sure it's thawed through and through. Clean and remove any pinfeathers; remove the giblets, neck, etc. Rinse with cold water. Pat dry. Brush with olive oil; rub down with black pepper and salt. Stuff the cavity with cut up oranges, apples, celery, green onions, leeks.

"Cover the bottom of the grill 3 coals deep and light them. Do this at least 1 hour before you start cooking. When the coals have turned ashy and there's a minimum of flames, you're ready to cook. Scatter a handful of wet hickory chips on top of the coals. Put the grill in place. Put the turkey in a sturdy metal roasting pan and place it on the grill. Put the cover on the grill. (By the way, make sure the cover fits over the turkey.) Leave the vents open by the coals, but close the vents on top. In a few minutes, smoke will start pouring out. This is good. Every $1/2$ hour or so add more hickory chips. If the coals start to die off, then open the vents in the lid for a few minutes. After an hour, the bird will be stained like a pensioner's dentures. This is also good. An 18-pound bird will take 5 to 6 hours, although if it takes longer, the bird will only taste better (cooking it at a lower heat tends to make it juicier). After 4 or 5 hours, insert a meat thermometer into the meaty part of the thigh (not the bone), and keep testing until it reads 180°F. When it's ready, take it off the fire immediately and let the bird sit for 15 minutes before carving. You can take drippings from the roasting pan. (Mmmmm!)"

Milo Burda's Amazing Bean Soup

Milo lived next door to me for three months, in an old apartment building across from the crazy Safeway in downtown Portland. He was sensitive and funny, and had the most incredible collection of dental molds I'd ever seen (the *only* collection of dental molds I've ever seen). He was also a fierce activist, and spent a lot of time making signs protesting various injustices and marching around the downtown mall. People who believe in something *and* act on it are so rare that I was completely captivated by his passion, transfixed by his charisma. Knowing Milo made me understand much about the meaning of the phrase "cult following."

Milo loved to cook, and would often make dinner for me and whichever homeless people he'd struck up a conversation with that day by the mall. As a result, he soon had a large group of people who would gather around and walk with him as he protested. It wasn't because they wanted a meal from him; they wanted *him*, wanted to spend time with him, to hear what he thought about things. This was eventually what drove us apart. I wanted to spend time with him, alone, not with three or ten or nineteen people who believed he was God. Milo thought me selfish for not opening *my* apartment to the hungry masses, but I considered my home relief from the world (cocktail waitressing gave me quite my fill of irritating behavior) and also had two rambunctious cats—in my mind, the place was full.

Soon at least ten people were sleeping on Milo's floor every night, and when the manager found out (I swear it was not me who told) he evicted him. Many of Milo's new friends made signs of protest but to no avail. The word on the street is that he moved to Seattle. He isn't lonely, I'm sure of that.

4 garlic cloves, chopped
1 onion, chopped
3^1/$_2$ cups vegetable broth
1 can garbanzo beans
1 can kidney beans
1 can lima beans
1 can pinto beans
^{1}/$_3$ cup brown sugar
2 teaspoons curry powder
4 teaspoons dried mustard
1 teaspoon red wine vinegar
Chopped spinach
   (use your own judgment
   as to the amount)
Chopped mushrooms

Sauté chopped garlic and onion in ^{1}/$_2$ cup vegetable broth in a heavy pan. Add the rest of the broth, then the beans (with juice). Add the sugar, curry powder, mustard, vinegar, spinach and mushrooms. Simmer for ^{1}/$_2$ hour, then serve the multitudes.

LEWIS'S 20-CLOVES-OF-GARLIC CHICKEN

Lewis's family and mine go way back. Lewis's father was my mother's first boyfriend at Camp Delaware, summer of '44, and though she caught him kissing Meryl Rollwagon behind the dining hall, they remained friends. It was hard not to: our grandfathers were raised in the same tiny town in Wisconsin a century ago, our grandmothers live next door to one another, and my mother and Lewis's mother (who is *not* Meryl Rollwagon) are the closest of friends. Our families celebrate Christmas together every year at Shim's Lotus Blossom Palace, feasting on Peking duck and other secular delights. Lewis and I never dated per se, although we have been slated for marriage since our diaper days. We have, however, been longtime friends, and I'm sure his presence in my life has been far more defining than many of the men I can more truthfully call ex-boyfriends. Lewis is someone with whom I can eat 20-Cloves-of-Garlic Chicken and not care what my breath smells like afterward. How many people can you say that about?

Preheat the oven to 375°F. Coat 4 chicken legs and 4 chicken thighs with 1/3 cup olive oil seasoned with salt, pepper and nutmeg. Place in a heavy casserole dish and add 1/6 cup white wine, 1/2 tablespoon tarragon and 2 diced celery stalks. Add 20 cloves of garlic, peeled, but left whole. Cover the casserole with a double layer of aluminum foil before putting on the lid. Bake for 1 1/2 hours.

Good things are coming to y...
course of time.
Lucky #: 05, 10, 16, 26, 34...

An empty stomach is not a good
political adviser.

This is the month when ingenuit...
stands high on the list.

You are a bundle of energy,
always on the go.
Lucky #: 10, 11, 25, 29...

A liar is not believed even though
he tell the truth.

VITO'S VEGGIE GALETTE

When I got off work the night Oscar essentially cheated on me in front of my face, I went to the Space Room—a dark, smoky bar notorious for its strong drinks—to chain-smoke and drown my sorrows in cheap martinis. I didn't want to talk to anyone and had already told two very drunk and red-faced men to "bug off," a phrase I never expected to fall from my mouth, when I looked up and saw a man at the other end of the bar who looked as forlorn as I did. He had taken the stir stick out of his drink and was poking it methodically into his cheek, and without thinking I yelled, "Hey, you, stop! You're going to poke your eye out!"

Vito raised his head and looked at me. What passed between us seemed like a flood of pure tenderness and wonder, although it was clearly something else entirely. I barely remember leaving my seat, but suddenly I was standing next to him, having grabbed his weapon and broken it in half.

He was a chef and had, that night, made a terrible, *terrible* mistake. He wouldn't tell me what it was, and not being a chef, it was hard for me to imagine what it might be. Had he poisoned someone? I never did find out. We spent the next couple of weeks moaning to each other about the various disappointments in our lives. It was cheaper than therapy, I suppose, and though I recognized our relationship for what it was, it still felt really, really nice.

We'd been dating for three weeks when I found out this book was going to be published. Vito was just as excited as I was about it, although for different reasons: He wanted one of his recipes to appear in the book.

"You're ready to be an ex-boyfriend?" I joked.

"Just make up a story, then use my recipe. But I want my name on it."

"You want your real name used?"

"Well, it's *my* recipe. I should get credit for it, shouldn't I?"

In the days that followed he made some of the most wonderful meals of my dating history trying to come up with the perfect recipe to publish, along with his name. My task was to write our (fictional) demise without mentioning that it was rather ridiculous that we were even together at all. I don't think we even made it one more week, but Vito got what he wanted, and here it is.

2 to 3 organic russet potatoes
1 carrot
1 yam
1 tablespoon minced garlic
1 tablespoon stone-ground mustard
Fresh parsley and thyme to taste
5 ounces cheese (a mix of white Cheddar, Gruyére and Fontina)
Vegetable oil and butter
Salt and pepper

Preheat the oven to 400°F. Grate the potatoes, carrot and yam into a bowl, and add the garlic, mustard and herbs. Drain off the juice in the bowl, but don't rinse. Heat 1 tablespoon of oil in a skillet, add half of the potato mixture and form a mound, then add 2 tablespoons of butter and pat into a 2-inch high cake. Add the cheese, top with the rest of the potato mixture and flip the cake when the bottom is crispy. Season to taste. Finish in the oven for 10 to 15 minutes. Extraordinary.

SOFTBALL CALVIN'S TUNA CASSEROLE

When I was in high school in New York, I used to play softball in Central Park on the weekends with a random group of people. There was a guy, Calvin, who lived in Jersey but drove his truck over the bridge every Saturday just for the game. We flirted like crazy, and then one day after a game he told me he had "an engagement" later that evening, and asked if he could come back to my house for a shower. I had biked to the field, so we put my bike in his truck and drove across town. My folks were away, and I probably don't have to tell you what his innocent shower turned into. When he left—far too late to make any sort of engagement he may, or may not, have actually had—we both forgot completely about my bike. (I should add here that it's more than a miracle that the bike was not stolen, unchained in the bed of his truck as it lay, and I used this good fortune to convince myself that letting Calvin come over wasn't really a terrible thing to have done since I had not been punished for it by a retributive god.) He dropped the bike off later that week, leaving it with the doorman with a note and his phone number taped to the seat. The next weekend I took the bus to the field and drove back to Jersey City with Calvin after the game. He cooked me tuna casserole because it was the only thing he knew how to make. He said his mother had made it for his father every Sunday night for twenty years. Then, later in the evening, he told me his parents had gotten

Here's the bike. Give me a call if you would like to have lunch or ~~dinner~~ sometime this week

divorced when he was three. "I thought she made it every Sunday for twenty years," I said. He was totally unfazed. "Oh, she did," he said. "She only lived a few blocks away. I used to carry it over to him, with a napkin and silverware and everything."

1 bag wide egg noodles or shells
1 can cream of mushroom soup
1 can tuna
1 can of those dried crispy onion things
1 cup peas or string beans
Pepper
Salt
Oregano

Preheat the oven to 375°F. Boil the noodles and leave them just a little firm. In an oven-safe pan, combine the noodles, soup, tuna, peas/beans and spices. Bake for 10 to 15 minutes. Add the crispy onions to the top and bake for another 5 minutes.

MEN

FERNANDA'S BOYFRIEND BERT'S HUNKY BRAN MUFFINS

I have to come clean on this and explain right off that Bert wasn't ever really my boyfriend. He was my housemate for a while, and he and my cat, Fernanda, were in love with each other. Try as I did to insinuate myself into Bert's bed, it was Fern who got to sleep with him every night. It was like being betrayed by your best friend, and I resented their love. Fortunately, Bert moved out after about six months to go battle forest fires in Yosemite, and Fernanda, to my great glee, forgot all about him. Despite his rejection of me in favor of a feline (who, admittedly, is gorgeous and has a bit of a licking fetish) I have harbored no great ill will toward Bert, possibly because of this muffin recipe. He baked them once a week, and though their preparation is a bit time-consuming, the result is a truly glorious hunky chunky muffin that is a meal unto itself. He let Fern lick the bowl when he was done, and sometimes I let her do it, too, and wonder if somewhere in her peabrain she remembers the muffin-baking man she once loved.

1 1/2 cups unprocessed wheat bran
1 1/4 cups whole wheat flour
1 1/4 teaspoons baking soda
Pinch of salt
Liberal dash of cinnamon
Handful of oats
Liberal sprinkle of wheat germ
1/4 cup honey
1/4 cup melted butter
1/4 cup molasses
2 eggs

Splash of vanilla extract
1 cup buttermilk
2 to 3 handfuls raw sunflower seeds
Handful or more chopped walnuts
Lots of raisins

Combine $1/2$ cup of the bran with $1/2$ cup boiling water, and let it steep. In a separate bowl, combine the rest of the bran with the flour, baking soda, salt, cinnamon, oats and wheat germ. In a third bowl—a big one, with a cover if you have one, so you can store the batter in it in the fridge overnight—blend together the honey and the butter. Add the eggs and molasses and vanilla. Then, to bowl number 1 (the steeping bran bowl) add the buttermilk. Now you've got 3 separate mixtures, and what you want to do is alternately add the flour mixture and the buttermilk mixture to the honey/butter mixture, beginning and ending with flour. Then add all the mix-ins until they're as hunky as you like 'em. Let the mixture sit, covered, in the fridge overnight. Bake the next morning in a preheated 400°F oven for 20 to 25 minutes.

The recipe usually makes between 9 and 12 muffins, depending on how much extra stuff you added and how big you like 'em. They also freeze really well and are great after a minute or so in the nuker.

NOTES